THE CREATIVE SEED

Lilian Wissink has over twenty years' experience in counselling and creating personal development programs. Assisting people to discover and realise their potential by helping them to develop compassionate self-awareness and new skills is fundamental to her philosophy — an approach that is further supported by her own experience as a developing artist. Over many years she has enjoyed creative expression in several different areas, including writing, acting, drawing, painting, photography, singing and dancing.

THE CREATIVE SEED

HOW TO ENRICH YOUR LIFE THROUGH CREATIVITY

LILIAN WISSINK BA GradDipCounselling

Empower

practical self-help tools by leading experts

First published 2013
This edition published 2020

Exisle Publishing Pty Ltd
PO Box 864, Chatswood, NSW 2057, Australia
226 High Street, Dunedin 9016, New Zealand
www.exislepublishing.com

A CiP record for this book is available from the National Library
of Australia.

ISBN 978-1-925820-30-0

Designed by Mark Thacker
Typeset in Miller Text Roman 9.5/14pt
Illustration on page 56 adapted from
Loopall @ Vectorstock.com

Printed in China

This book uses paper sourced under ISO 14001 guidelines from
well-managed forests and other controlled sources.

10 9 8 7 6 5 4 3 2 1

Disclaimer
While this book is intended as a general information resource
and all care has been taken in compiling the contents, this
book does not take account of individual circumstances.
Neither the author nor the publisher and their distributors can
be held responsible for any loss, claim or action that may arise
from reliance on the information contained in this book.

Note
The names and some of the details of the people mentioned
in the case studies have been changed to protect their privacy..

In loving memory of my inventive,
creative Pappie, Antonius

CONTENTS

Preface

IS THIS BOOK FOR YOU?

- Do you feel there is more to discover about yourself?
- Do you have an inkling that there is some form of creative expression you would like to try? Writing? Singing? Painting? Playing a musical instrument? Sculpture? Perhaps an avenue of craft, such as woodturning, leadlighting, ceramics or creative knitting and crocheting?
- Do you regret not having pursued an earlier creative interest?
- Do you remember the enjoyment of being creative and playful when you were younger and want to tap into that pleasure again?
- Do you already have an interest in or a fascination with some form of creative expression but are not sure how to go about developing it?
- Do you get discouraged when the challenges of life seem to get in the way of you moving forward in your creative expression?
- Are you active in a particular creative domain but experience self-doubt, frustration and other obstacles that thwart your progress?

If you said 'Yes' to any of these questions then it's time for you to let *The Creative SEED* guide you on your path. I will take you on a journey to explore your creative-self and find ways to expand your current sense of what you believe you can do. This journey is lifelong and once embraced will enrich and inspire you. Each chapter has questions and exercises to help you move forward. These exercises are designed to increase your self-awareness — the key to unlocking your creative spark. What you discover will help you to deal with any obstacles that get in your way. All creative and performing artists experience obstacles, no matter the stage of their journey — the challenges of self-doubt, fear, anxiety, procrastination and frustration. What makes you successful is your determination to keep going, to keep learning and staying active in your creative expression. You'll learn helpful ways to handle challenges and will find that your creative skills will reach a new, exciting dimension you had not thought possible.

A BRIEF OUTLINE

Chapter One in Part One is written especially for readers who are not sure about the area of creativity they would like to explore. You'll have the opportunity to discover what is likely to be exciting and satisfying. Even if you are established in an avenue of creative expression, this chapter provides insight into other forms of creativity you might enjoy. Myths surrounding creativity are also discussed as a means to understanding how beliefs influence your approach to creative expression. The last chapter (Chapter Four) in Part One provides a clear overview of what the creative process is all about. Whether you write, sing, paint or sculpt; whether you knit, turn wood or make pots — in all creative pursuits, you will go through stages, face challenges and solve problems along the way.

Part Two helps you to explore and develop your creative expression. Presented in this section are ways to support and guide you through the common ups and downs of the creative process so that you can reach realistic and exciting goals.

You will read stories of people who are just like you — discovering and nurturing their creative-self. These are people I have met over the years in my profession as a counselling psychologist and in workshops and classes that I have taken as a developing artist.

PROVEN STRATEGIES THAT MOVE YOU FORWARD

The strategies in this book are based on sound, well-researched theories of Cognitive Behaviour Theory (CBT), Transactional Analysis (TA) and mindfulness. A major premise of CBT is that the way we think influences how we feel and behave. This book provides straightforward strategies to help you deal with any unhelpful thoughts and behaviours that thwart your potential. TA also underpins my writing. This theory is particularly helpful in understanding the different aspects of our personality and how they interact. And thirdly, the philosophy of mindfulness helps you to become more present-centred rather than caught up in worries about the past or concerns for the future. At the core of mindfulness is self-acceptance and compassion, both crucial in any part of our lives, including our journey into creativity.

KEEPING A JOURNAL

Keeping a journal is a helpful tool. An unlined art diary is ideal for this purpose. I hope you will use it to do the exercises offered to you throughout this book. You can express the feelings that bubble away at various times and write down ideas, desires or frustrations. You can write poetry or prose, sketch or doodle. Your journal can be a history of your experience and a place to honour your strengths. Keep it private, as this will encourage you to feel free to express yourself in whatever way you choose.

HOW TO READ THIS BOOK

There are several different ways you can read this book. You could dip into it at random, but I suggest you read it from start to finish and notice the chapters and exercises to which you particularly relate. Then come back and read more slowly, giving yourself time to do the exercises. Each exercise is valuable in helping you to understand yourself more clearly and find ways to move forward creatively. However, don't feel you have to do every exercise in the order it is presented. Go with your gut feeling. You will know, for example, if you need particular help with procrastination or perhaps in dealing with stress in your life. So go with what you believe will be most helpful to begin with. This is a guidebook and a workbook. Keep coming back to it. Use it time and time again to inspire you to keep going in your creative life.

So let's begin.

PART ONE

DISCOVERING YOUR CREATIVE-SELF

Chapter One

WHO IS MY CREATIVE-SELF?

Imagination is the beginning of creation.
You imagine what you desire,
you will what you imagine
and at last you create what you will.

— GEORGE BERNARD SHAW

You may already enjoy an avenue of creative expression or perhaps you have never seriously considered the idea but now feel tempted to explore the possibilities. Maybe secretly you would like to look into some form of creativity but you keep thinking it's not that important or you don't have the time. This chapter takes you through some exercises that will provide ideas to inspire you. You have the opportunity to discover something unique about yourself and see that creativity is already a part of your life. So set aside some quiet time to explore the answers in your journal. If you are not used to journalling in this way, just start with a few words, ideas or symbols. As time goes on it's likely you will feel more comfortable and see that expressing your thoughts and feelings helps you to understand yourself better and clarify things you want to do.

YOUR SKILLS AND QUALITIES

We all have skills and personal qualities that we develop over time. Maybe you work in a supermarket and know how to chat to customers, check through groceries or manage the ordering of stock. Perhaps you have reared children, taught at tertiary level, driven a bus or taxi, or worked in a hospital or successful business and have fine-tuned a whole host of skills to carry out your work. Not just your skills, but also your unique qualities have helped you in many different roles. These qualities may include persistence, time management, compassion, efficiency, determination and many other attributes that you have developed over the years. It might surprise you to learn that you can draw on any or all of these qualities to expand into a new area of your life.

We create every day. For example, we cook a delicious dinner, write a business proposal or fix a leaking roof. How we go about these everyday tasks gives us insight into what is needed for other forms of creativity. You may be asking how fixing a leaking roof can be anything like learning to play the guitar or learning how to paint. Well, lots of things are common to both: you need to have the tools, set aside time, think about what to do, have a go, fix up your mistakes and maybe ask for help. For now, acknowledge that you already accomplish many things that require thought, imagination, experimentation and determination.

Let's read about Sarah and see how she acknowledged her skills and qualities. Then it will be your turn.

SARAH

Sarah is a part-time physiotherapist. She is happily married, with three children who have now all left home. Over the past couple of years she has noticed periods of feeling down and dissatisfied about her life. She wants to find something enjoyable that is different from her usual activities. She isn't really sure what she would like to do, but she is willing to give herself some time to think about the possibilities. When Sarah thinks about her skills and qualities, she remembers how she went about redecorating the lounge room on a modest budget. This is what she writes in her journal:

Skills:

- I researched what colours went well with my favourite colour yellow that I wanted to highlight in the room.
- I experimented with different shades by painting them on boards.
- I learnt how to make cushion covers and enlisted the help of my sister.
- I invested in some good quality brushes to help me do the job.
- I asked for feedback about my idea to do a feature wall.

It is a little harder for Sarah to think of her personal qualities because of her modesty. But after a while she realises that in order to redecorate the lounge room she drew on the following qualities:

Qualities:

- Imagination to play with different ideas.
- Ingenuity in deciding colour scheme.
- Courage to take risks and ask for help.
- Determination to keep going even when it all seemed too hard.
- Playfulness in making some funky looking cushions.

After Sarah finished this exercise she felt more confident that she could try something new, like drawing and painting. She realised that she had developed lots of skills over the years. Although not successful straightaway, with time and determination she accomplished what she set out to do — and she had fun and enjoyment along the way! You can do this too. Now it's your turn to think about the skills and qualities you already have.

YOUR SKILLS AND QUALITIES

Think about something you have accomplished recently. It can be big or small. Give yourself some time and in your journal write about the skills and qualities that helped you achieve what you set out to do. Don't be bashful! Some people find it difficult to acknowledge their positives. If this is true for you, begin with a few words such as: 'I made a start by ...'

How did you go? You can come back to this exercise at any time. You might find that things come to you as you get on with your day and you give yourself time to reflect. But keep coming back to it. Once you explore one accomplishment why not find another? This exercise is valuable in boosting your creative self-esteem.

The next two exercises are adapted from a book called *Live the Life You Love* by a careers counsellor, Barbara Sher. These exercises help you identify activities and experiences that uniquely give you pleasure, enjoyment and a buzz for life. Why is this important? Well, it can propel you to make choices about what you might like to explore creatively.

CREATIVITY IN CHILDHOOD

In your journal, write down the different activities you enjoyed when you were little. What did you love to do? These activities can be big or small, from reading books to putting on plays for family and friends, from making a billycart to riding your bike, from building things with wood to playing in autumn leaves. Don't censor yourself when you write your list. Be free and jot down everything you can think of. Write down the activities on one side of the page and on the other side write down what it was about each activity you liked. What senses were stimulated? For example, if you enjoyed making mud pies you might say something like: 'I liked the feeling of mud and moisture squelching through my fingers. I liked decorating the pies with leaves and berries.' Or if you enjoyed playing with puppets you might say something like: 'I liked how a story would unfold with the puppets talking to each other. I liked the excitement of seeing how it would end.' Get the idea? Have a play with your list and see what you come up with.

Sometimes it's difficult to remember our childhood. If this is the case for you, that's okay. The other exercises in this chapter will also provide opportunities to explore possible creative paths.

Here are just a few of the things that Sarah wrote:

As a child:

Activity	Why I liked it
Drawing and colouring in	Making things look pretty
Dress-ups	Fantasy, making up stories
Made-up plays	Liked pretending, fun
Dancing	Felt free and happy
Swinging on the swing and singing	Felt like I was in another world
Watching father develop photos	Felt magical, something appears out of nothing

After completing this exercise you may feel a sense of nostalgia or even a sense of loss. Or you may feel excited or inspired to feel the pleasure of these past activities once again. Gently accept whatever feelings emerge. It can be helpful to write about your feelings in your journal or to draw or doodle. Perhaps you discovered some interest or fascination that has been lost for some years. How about choosing a couple of activities on your list and trying them out again now, as an adult? Just for fun! See how you feel.

CREATIVITY IN ADULTHOOD

Write down the things you love to do now and that you have enjoyed over the years of being an adult, even if you haven't had a lot of time to engage in these activities. Once again, don't censor yourself. They might be social activities such as dancing, or aspects of your work such as organising a function, or playing sport. Again, write down the activities on one side of the page and then on the other side write down what it is that you particularly like about doing this activity.

Here are some of Sarah's examples:

As an adult:

Activity	Why I liked it
Making bread	Sense of accomplishment
Running	Felt strong and independent
Singing	Liked being expressive, joyful
Acting	Fantasy, being someone else
Sewing and knitting	Making something useful out of material

When you have completed the last two exercises, take some time to look at *why* you enjoyed the activities in your childhood and as an adult. Do you notice any neglected pleasures or ones you have just forgotten about? Can you notice any themes? Sarah realised that when she was young and again later as an adult she enjoyed activities where she used her imagination and could be expressive.

Whatever you discovered by doing these two exercises I hope you are starting to gather a stronger picture of what you might like to explore. What we enjoy and value influences the life choices we make. Sometimes we get sidetracked into activities and even careers because of expectations from others or society. Or perhaps we have a heightened sense of duty or need to conform. Now it's time to do something that reflects your inner drive.

Values

Values are the important principles that guide our life. They include personal qualities and strengths we respect within ourselves and other people, and also the qualities we wish to develop. Values echo how we want to function as a human being and they give meaning and purpose to our lives. Your values need to be in line with your creative interests, so it's important to think about your values as you explore and develop your creative expression.

Values are different to goals. Goals are specific things that we want to achieve, and we will focus on goals in later chapters. Values guide us in making decisions and achieving our goals. We often don't give much thought to our values but they run deep within us. If we live our life outside our value system we are likely to become unhappy and dissatisfied. This is what happened to Tan.

TAN

Tan immigrated to Australia with his family from Thailand when he was a teenager. He had always been encouraged by his parents to work hard and earn good money. He followed their advice and worked in a bank. Tan is a brilliant creative problem solver and inspires those around him. Management, however, didn't acknowledge his creative spark. Slowly his zest for his work diminished.

Besides valuing creativity in the workplace, Tan recently acknowledged other deeply held values: his musicality and love of composition. He had pushed these values aside but eventually he decided to take a risk and undertake a degree in music, despite his parents' concerns. He realised that working in the financial sector was gradually depressing him. It took courage to make such a change, particularly as it meant leaving a well-paid job. Although Tan is only halfway through his course, his enthusiasm for life has returned and he is excited about his future.

The following exercise helps you think about your values and encourages you to reflect on whether you are living your life according to these values. This exercise also helps you to link your values to any creative path that you've thought about. If you are already pursuing a creative life, hopefully you will see that these values are embedded in your creative expression and other parts of your life.

PERSONAL CREATIVE VALUES

There are many values and below is a list of a few. Read through the list and tick the ones that are the most important to you, especially in regard to your creativity. Feel free to add any other values you like to the list.

contribution	*expanding knowledge*	*wealth*
accomplishment	*contribution to society*	*fitness*
adventure	*fun*	*truth*
beauty	*authenticity*	*ideas*
competition	*freedom*	*history*
courage	*acknowledgment*	*challenge*

caring	*open-mindedness*	*curiosity*
artistry	*self-expression*	*nature*
flexibility	*success*	*being free*
acceptance	*working alone*	*sensuality*
fairness	*working with others*	*colour*
imagination	*excitement*	*compassion*
playfulness	*originality*	

Take some time to look at the values you ticked. When you are ready, write down your top six values — the ones that are really important to you. Are these values related to what you once enjoyed or what you enjoy now? Think about which value is most closely linked to what you enjoyed as a child. Which value is most closely linked to what you enjoy as an adult?

Let's go back to Sarah who wants to draw and paint. This is what she listed as her top six values:

- Accomplishment
- Beauty
- Enjoyment
- Colour
- Expression
- Open-mindedness

Sarah also realised that her values have changed over the years. When she was younger her values centred on helping others and she experienced satisfaction in being a physiotherapist and a mother. Now she realises that some other values are pushing forward to be recognised and need to be nurtured. This surprised her. Perhaps this may happen to you.

Hopefully by doing the above four exercises you have discovered what's important to you, what stimulates you and gives you pleasure. If you are still not sure, that's okay. Exploration in itself is a worthwhile experience. The next exercise will help too. It's a fantasy exercise. Fantasising is fun and gives us insight into what we truly desire and want for ourselves. So give yourself permission to be free and discover whatever comes to mind as you let your imagination roam.

CREATE A MAGICAL DAY

Imagine that you are in a magical land and you can play in any creative realm. There is no one here to judge you. What do you see yourself 'trying out' on this day? Might you splash paint on a canvas and create a vivid landscape? Be the lead singer in a rock band? Dance with abandon? Create or act out exciting characters for a play or novel? Here you can fantasise without worrying about the practical challenges of how to go about expressing yourself creatively. For now you are just playing in your imagination. So enjoy!

Allow yourself to do this fantasy again in an hour's time or in a day or two. It will be interesting to see if other ideas emerge. Notice if you step in quickly and put up barriers or create fear: 'No, I couldn't possibly learn to dance, that's only for young people. I'd feel stupid going to classes. Forget it.' If this happens, be aware of how your mind sets up these barriers. Later chapters will show you how to deal with them. For now all you need is a willingness to continue on the journey.

Are you developing some ideas about what area of creativity you would like to explore? Or maybe you know already. Whatever creative pursuit and whatever stage you are up to, exploration, experimentation and playfulness are essential. So begin something creative today. Keep an open mind and be curious. Relax and enjoy exploring. If these are your first attempts they will most likely be raw, so don't be harsh and critical of yourself. *Give yourself permission to be a beginner.* You can start by reflecting on what you enjoy or what you are intrigued by in life, as this can stimulate ideas about what you might like to draw, paint, make or write about. Perhaps you love being outdoors, so look closely at the colours, textures and the shapes about you. Tune into how you feel. Maybe you love reading detective stories, so think about an interesting or unusual character. Consider what engages you about this character? Whether you are just starting or have had some experience in your creative domain, think about some playful activities to try out.

Here are some ideas:
- Write about the most exciting day in your life.
- Pick an object in your kitchen and draw it.
- Collect pictures in books that inspire you and create a scrapbook.
- Play music you enjoy and dance to it.
- Sing a song each day.
- Be a character in a play or film and think and act how he/she would talk about a particular subject at a dinner party.
- Find your old school recorder and play it.
- Mould clay or plasticine into whatever you like.

And now it's your turn. In your journal brainstorm a list of creative activities and then choose one to start with. Go on and have a go. You can then write or draw about your experience if you wish.

YOUR CREATIVITY MAY REVEAL MORE THAN YOU THINK

It's interesting to contemplate how your creative-self is relevant and important in your life. 'Why do I want to sing/paint/write, etc?' 'What's in it for me to pursue this?' The answers to these questions are illuminating and sometimes not what you expect. Our creativity is not only about the act of writing/painting/ singing/dancing, but also about the bigger picture of how we are in the world or how we want to be in the world. Let me explain with a personal example. A few years ago, just for fun, I did some singing workshops. I had always believed I could not sing and told myself the usual negative things: 'I've got a terrible voice — I'm tone deaf.' But I went on a wonderful journey and found my voice over a period of several months. This culminated in belting out a couple of songs at a local club. Wow! What a thrill to sing Joe Cocker's 'The Letter' dressed in tight jeans and a leather jacket! In one of our weekly workshops we were asked the question, 'How is my "singer" relevant to me and my life?' This is what I wrote in my journal: 'She is showing me my voice — she is giving me permission to express myself. She is finding a way to express what I have always hidden — my voice.' This did not just mean my singing voice but a voice to express myself in many different ways, including drawing, painting and writing. So in your journal give yourself some time to express why it's important for you to pursue some form of creativity. What do you hope to discover? Remember that you can write in different ways or you can doodle or draw symbols or images. It's up to you.

CREATIVE TOUCHSTONES

This chapter has given you the opportunity to explore:

- skills and qualities you already possess
- what you enjoyed as a child and how this may hold the key to what you might love to do now
- what you enjoy doing as an adult, which will also provide clues to your creative gifts
- the personal values that are meaningful to you and guide your life; these values give you a sense of purpose as well as underpin the area of creativity that might ultimately satisfy you the most
- the areas of creativity you are ready to play with.

Chapter Two

WHAT IS CREATIVITY?

*I am always doing that which I cannot do,
in order that I may learn how to do it.*

— PABLO PICASSO

We all know the word 'creative', but few of us actually attach that word to ourselves or what we do. Instead we are coaxed into believing the opinion so often brandished about in our society that you either have 'it' or you don't. By believing such a myth we limit ourselves and could miss an opportunity to develop a new, fulfilling dimension to our lives. In this chapter, six common myths are explored to help you unravel your ideas about creativity. Why is this important? Our beliefs are like the paddles of a canoe and they steer us in a particular direction. Sometimes beliefs support and guide us and sometimes they muddy what we truly want for ourselves. So it helps to sort out our ideas and challenge any that get in the way of our potential satisfaction and happiness.

MYTHS SURROUNDING CREATIVITY

The next exercise lists six statements for you to ponder. Give yourself time to think about whether you agree or not. Maybe do the washing up or go for a walk while you mull things over. Do something in the first instance that doesn't require you to talk with others. Allow yourself to reflect on how these ideas influence you.

WHAT YOU THINK

Myth 1: You must be born with a special gift to be creative.
Myth 2: Creativity is an escape and secondary to other pursuits such as having a well-paid job.
Myth 3: Creative people have a touch of madness in them.
Myth 4: Creativity is a mystical, mysterious journey that only a few people undertake.
Myth 5: To be successful in a creative area you must start early in life.
Myth 6: You must have passion to be creative.

After reflecting on these six statements, write in your journal about any that catch your attention. Write about how these myths influence your approach to creative expression. You can write a few words or many. It's up to you. Remember there are no 'shoulds' about how you write or draw in your journal. If you feel reluctant, just start with a few words or symbols to reflect what you believe.

Was it easy for you to simply agree or not agree with these statements or were some perhaps not that black or white? Could any of these beliefs be getting in the way of you exploring and enjoying an avenue of creative expression? Most people discover that some of the above views are things they think or say in one way or another. Why not have a talk to family and friends and see what they think? As you read this book you will find that what you think has quite an influence on what you actually do. The good news is that, if you want, you can learn to think differently and this will dramatically shape how you live your life and create. Let's look at each statement in turn.

MYTH 1:
You must be born with a special gift to be creative

We are all born creative. Think of how you played as a child. Did you play dress-ups or enjoy imaginary games? Perhaps you put on concerts for family and friends. Maybe you constructed secret hideouts in the garden or played indoor cricket with paddle pop sticks? Did you have imaginary friends, make up fantasy stories or pretend you were in a pop band? If it's difficult to think of how you played as a child, perhaps you can find opportunities to watch children play in real life or even on television. When considering childhood play you can see that the activities require imagination and effort. You also need to think things through and solve some problems along the way. These are all key elements in the creative process. Certainly some people are born with a genetic predisposition for a particular creative talent and we might call this a special gift. However, if they don't have the desire or the commitment to nurture their gift their talent remains unused. What is more important than innate talent is the willingness to explore what interests and excites us and to have the courage to deal with the inevitable challenges that come our way — just as we do in any part of life. As you nurture your creativity you encourage and develop a part of yourself that is innate. It might have been buried or left untouched for years, but it is there. Creativity is at the core of our being and has a yearning to be recognised and nurtured. Creativity is essentially about freedom: the freedom to express some aspect of ourselves as yet untapped. To nourish this part of ourselves is a *special gift*.

MYTH 2:
Creativity is an escape and secondary to more important pursuits such as having a well-paid job

To say creativity is an escape really belittles what it's about. An escape from what? Some people say spending time on creative expression, such as writing or painting, is an escape from the more important things in life, like work. Our culture places a high value on having a successful career and money to buy things that are said to make us feel successful and happy. But we can get carried away with these values at the expense of doing other things we love. And work and different forms of creative expression are not necessarily exclusive. We can do both — work *and* sing/paint/write/sculpt — *or* choose to focus on one. Let's also look at 'escape' in another way. Creativity can be a very positive escape. It can be an escape from boredom, sadness and perhaps other difficulties in life that you need to take a break from. This sounds very valuable to me!

MYTH 3:
Creative people have a touch of madness in them

Even though over the centuries there have been examples of creative people who have suffered from mental illness, there is no evidence that creativity stems from this state. Rather, people learn to cope with their disorder and create in spite of it. Van Gogh suffered from mental illness, but despite his debilitating symptoms, he pushed through to honour and express his creative-self and to become one of the great artists in history — although sadly he didn't know that in his lifetime. We may suffer from depression or anxiety, or experience emotional distress, but to stimulate our mind with what fascinates us can be a healing balm for the difficulties we experience. Our painful feelings of grief, anger and jealousy can also provide a rich impetus for creative expression. Consider the love songs that have been written after a break-up.

MYTH 4:
Creativity is a mystical, mysterious journey that only a few people undertake

Creativity has been researched extensively and can be clearly understood from a logical and rational perspective rather than revered as something mystical. Experts see creativity as a learnt ability to experiment time and time again and to problem solve until we get to a desired outcome. This process is practical, not mysterious. Many creators, however, do acknowledge that something intangible occurs when their creativity flows. They feel they are more alive and connected to their true self. Depending on your belief system you might call this mystical, spiritual or magical.

Ken Robinson, a present day guru on creativity, sees it as creating something original that has value. In order to achieve originality, however, you need curiosity, persistence and a willingness to think outside the square and try something different. The more skilled we are with our creative tools, the more chance there is that our creativity will flourish. This is a journey that you can take.

MYTH 5:
To be successful in a creative area you have to start early in life

Again this belief is limiting. It's not about how old you are but about the time and the energy you give to your creative expression. You can start at the age of ten, thirty, sixty or later! Many people might have been caught up with careers and families for a long time, but as these commitments become less all-consuming, feel a yearning to explore something different. Let's turn this myth around and say that being older has advantages because of the life experiences and wisdom you have gathered over the years. What's more important than age is your willingness to learn the skills, to experiment and play. Each person's definition of 'successful' is different. For some, it might be learning how to express yourself artistically for your own pleasure and satisfaction — and this is perfectly valid. For others it might be to gain recognition in some way, such as getting a book published. There are many 'late bloomers'. Remember Susan Boyle's rise to fame in *Britain's Got Talent*? Raymond Chandler didn't write his first short story and novel until he was forty-five. Grandma Moses started painting in her seventies. Minnie Pwerle, one of Australia's highest selling contemporary artists, started painting in her eighties. British actor Liz Smith began her professional career in her fifties and continued well into her eighties. Exploring and enjoying some form of creative expression in later life is also an enjoyable way to stimulate your mind and heighten your sense of wellbeing.

MYTH 6:
You must have passion to be creative

Creative passion often conjures up an image of an expressive and colourful artist or a writer who is totally consumed by what they do. Perhaps even tormented. This image can be scary if you are beginning somewhat warily on your creative journey, and it can be misleading if you are already enjoying some form of creative expression but don't feel such intense emotion.

The emotions that accompany creativity vary and are reflective of our general personality, life events and current circumstances. We can have feelings that are mild such as interest and curiosity or strong emotions such as enthusiasm and excitement and, yes, stronger emotions such as passion. Emotions, including passion, can wax and wane and they do not need to be constant for creativity to bloom. We can also think of passion in two ways: healthy passion and unhealthy passion.

We experience healthy passion when we are enthusiastic and have an intense desire to focus on our art, writing, craft or performance activity. We might find it hard to think of other things or want to do other things because our desire and eagerness is so strong. There is often an obsessive quality to this kind of passion. Experiencing passion is exciting, but can easily tip over the edge into unhealthy passion where there is a loss of control that can lead to myriad negative consequences for our health and relationships. A distant cousin of mine is a gifted and driven artist and has recently had a sell-out exhibition. He has also lost his partner, alienated his children and developed a stress-related illness. His passion has blinded his need for exercise, healthy diet, adequate sleep and time for relationships.

Don't feel you *must* be passionate at the start of your creative journey or that you *must* sustain passion to be creative. Allow your feelings of interest, curiosity and fascination to guide you to explore and develop your creative interests. And if you do experience passion, enjoy the energy and the gift of this passion, but make sure it isn't at the expense of other important parts of your life.

A PERSONAL JOURNEY

Creativity is personal. You might downplay your creativity by saying, 'Oh, lots of people have painted landscapes before, written poetry or taken photos of the beautiful ocean,' but *your* approach is unique. Sure, if you are a beginner, what you create may well be raw but it is your creation. About twelve years ago I felt a tiny tug of inspiration to draw. There I was in my mid forties, not having drawn since I was about ten, nor having given any consideration to the idea of drawing or painting since that time. I sat down to draw a jug on the kitchen table and what came out was misshapen, flat and without form. But somehow I was touched by the actual experience and did not stop. I have encouraged myself to continue through the ups and downs of drawing and then painting over the past decade. Drawing that first jug was my creation. It was something I had not done before. I now value and treasure those early awkward drawings as my start as a visual artist.

THE ACTION IN CREATIVITY

Being creative is something you *do* rather than something you *are*. You might have a wonderful imagination, but unless you are willing to experiment and express yourself in some way, your imagination and creativity lie dormant. Even if you have some doubts, I know from my own experience and from watching many others that when you stay engaged in your creativity you will grow in competence and confidence. You will reap the satisfaction and the joy and discover the unimaginable. Many people have done so already. You can do it too.

CREATIVE TOUCHSTONES

We carry around ideas that influence how we view and approach creative expression. By acknowledging these beliefs I hope you have discovered what's helpful to keep and what needs to be discarded or at least heartily challenged.

Remember:
- We all have the gift of creativity and it's up to us to unwrap and nurture this gift.
- It's never too late to start.
- Creativity is a journey that begins with an interest and willingness to experience and experiment with something new.
- This journey is enjoyable, challenging and ultimately brings us closer to our deepest nature.

Chapter Three

YOUR STORY SO FAR ...

*To stimulate creativity, one must develop the
childlike inclination to play ...*

— ALBERT EINSTEIN

In the first chapter you gained insight into activities that gave you pleasure and satisfaction. And I hope some still do. This chapter provides an opportunity to reflect on key events that have shaped your life so far. You'll be able to explore what was inspiring and encouraging, and also acknowledge what wasn't helpful in providing the freedom to express yourself creatively. Understanding your story so far, with an attitude of acceptance and compassion, lays a foundation for creative development. Later in the chapter I'll expand on the importance of self-compassion, but for now think of it as being your own best friend.

SOME HISTORICAL INSIGHTS

It's often interesting to reflect on our personal history and what has influenced the direction of our life. Perhaps you have been focused on education, employment, paying the mortgage, family life, community work or travel. Maybe this is the first time you have given yourself the space to think of what else you would like to do in your life — something different, something creative. This is what happened to Sally, who had a satisfying life but, in her fifties, wanted to try something new.

SALLY

Sally remembers a happy childhood, growing up with her twin brother, Jeff. Her parents worked hard to provide them both with lots of opportunities to try out different activities: tennis, kids' theatre, swimming and music. Sally and Jeff enjoyed school and their childhood. They were both good 'all rounders'. Jeff became a solicitor and Sally completed an administration course and joined a medical practice as a receptionist. She worked for four years, before marrying and having a child, Rebecca. Her husband Tom was a schoolteacher. For over thirty years they lived in various country towns as Tom gained experience and seniority in the education system. Sally was content being involved in the different communities they lived in, enjoying part-time work and bringing up their daughter. Of course, there were ups and downs over the years, but at fifty-six Sally reflected that so far she'd had a good life. She felt a little confused and even guilty that now she wanted something different. She reluctantly admitted to herself that she had been swept along by circumstances, such as Tom's need to move frequently for his career. Now with her daughter and grandchildren far away, she felt lost and wanted to do something just for herself.

I suggested to Sally that she do a timeline to reflect the twists and turns that had been significant in her life, and to include any memories that influenced her creativity. I also asked Sally to extend her timeline into the future and write down her creative dreams and desires. You can see that by doing this exercise Sally became excited about two particular creative ideas.

Here is a snapshot of Sally's timeline:

Memories and events

Auntie Joan gave me a guitar for Christmas and I had lessons for two years.

Choreographed a dance routine for my friends for a dance competition.

Two friends said nasty things.

Had a one off experience playing in a band due to the regular player being ill.

AGE 12 13 15

Excited about the gift and enjoyed learning and playing over many years until Rebecca was born. Things got too busy to play.

Felt sad. Mum and Dad were kind and supportive, but I felt that dancing wasn't my 'thing'.

I wanted to do this again at some stage, but never did. Felt I should focus on schoolwork.

Feelings and thoughts

Memories and events

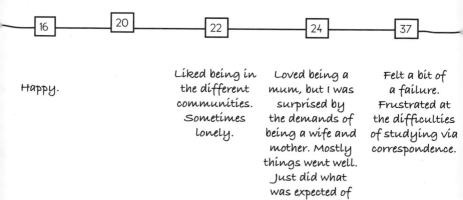

Moved to
Walgett.

We moved to
seven different
towns over the
next twenty
years.

Left
school
and met
Tom.

Got married.

Rebecca
was born.

Enrolled
in uni, but
withdrew
after a
year.

| 16 | 20 | 22 | 24 | 37 |

Happy.

Liked being in
the different
communities.
Sometimes
lonely.

Loved being a
mum, but I was
surprised by
the demands of
being a wife and
mother. Mostly
things went well.
Just did what
was expected of
me I guess.

Felt a bit of
a failure.
Frustrated at
the difficulties
of studying via
correspondence.

Feelings and thoughts

Memories and events

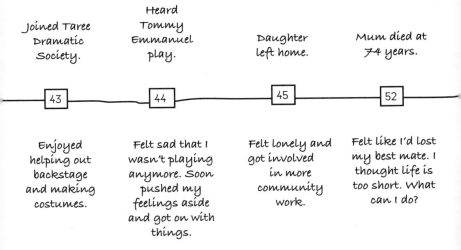

Joined Taree Dramatic Society.

Heard Tommy Emmanuel play.

Daughter left home.

Mum died at 74 years.

43

44

45

52

Enjoyed helping out backstage and making costumes.

Felt sad that I wasn't playing anymore. Soon pushed my feelings aside and got on with things.

Felt lonely and got involved in more community work.

Felt like I'd lost my best mate. I thought life is too short. What can I do?

Feelings and thoughts

DREAMS AND DESIRES

Play the guitar again. Maybe write some songs.

GOAL

Find my old guitar and sheet music in the shed and have a play.

In doing the timeline Sally reflected that, although she'd had a happy life, she had easily gone along with what others expected of her. What came as a complete suprise, while walking her dog the day after doing the timeline, was a memory of being at a birthday party when she was five or six. She couldn't remember whose party it was, but she did remember the crowded room where the parents and children gathered. She remembered pretending to be Goldilocks and another little friend playing the baby bear. In her mind she could see the people clapping and cheering and how happy this made her. Clearly this memory had emerged as a result of doing the timeline and she felt inspired to take out some plays from the local library and read them. She enjoyed the experience of letting herself be the characters. Sally is now playing her guitar and writing songs with a friend. She is also rehearsing for a local production of *Who's Afraid of Virginia Woolf*. The timeline unearthed creative avenues to explore. So who knows what you might discover by doing your own.

MY TIMELINE

Just as Sally did in the example, draw a line across the length of a page in your journal. Start with your early life and move across the page as your life continues. Leave some space for fantasies, dreams or goals. Above the line, write down any significant events that steered your life in a particular direction. These events might involve people, accomplishments, happy or difficult times or a change in circumstances. Also write down memories related to your creativity. Include your age or approximate age.

Below the line write down a few words that reflect how you generally felt at the time. Feel free to use colour and symbols if you wish.

> *Next, write down any dreams or desires you have for your creative future. It's okay to be vague and general. In later chapters you will learn how to bring these fantasies into focus and how to work towards them. If, however, you already have some specific goals in mind, write these down too.*

Give yourself some time to reflect on the events that have shaped your life. Can you see any patterns or themes emerging? Perhaps certain feelings came up as you recollected earlier times. Often our memories are fleeting and attached to feelings that are sometimes uncomfortable, but giving yourself time to be reflective is important in understanding your creative-self. Remember to use your journal to express any leftover feelings and thoughts after doing your timeline.

EARLY MESSAGES

The next exercise expands your understanding of your timeline by focusing specifically on the 'messages' related to creativity that you received from significant people in your past. Significant people may include parents, grandparents, teachers, friends, peer groups and even institutions like a church. The messages can be things people said out loud, such as: 'Wow! You're a great drawer!' or 'You can't sing dear, you're tone deaf.' Or the messages might have been conveyed through body language or what was 'allowed' or 'not allowed' in your home, school or peer group. For example, your parents might have criticised rock singers on television and you picked up that it would not be okay for you to sing rock songs or play the drums. Perhaps you remember your friends at school ridiculing others who liked to dance or draw, but secretly this was what you wanted to do.

I'd like to tell you about Jamal from South Africa. I first met Jamal when he was a university student studying accountancy. Despite working hard he struggled with his studies. From time to time he expressed his interest in art, but quickly dismissed this as being foolish. After graduating he went back to South Africa to work in his father's firm. Jamal kept in touch over the years and I was excited to hear about his change of direction.

JAMAL

Jamal worked as an accountant for several years after he graduated. Jamal's father was also an accountant and his mother worked as a secretary in a law firm. While Jamal was growing up his parents often said art was a waste of time and forced him to spend time on his schoolwork. Jamal remembers a scene when his father found him drawing and tore up his picture. He remembers feeling the pressure of being the eldest son and the responsibility of following in his father's footsteps. Jamal also remembers positive times when he enjoyed art at school and received encouragement from a particular teacher. However, the strong influence of his parents' messages led Jamal to abandon his art in secondary school and pursue the career his father had chosen for him.

In his mid thirties he was given responsibility for a branch of his father's firm in a new city. Away from his parents, with new friends and opportunities, his desire for artistic expression once again emerged. He felt guilty at first and that he was being foolish (a leftover message from his father), but slowly he learnt to let these negative beliefs go and with the encouragement of others he eventually sought out classes and went further with his artistic dreams.

Jamal now works part time and is in his second year of a Fine Arts degree. He has even sold two paintings. Despite the initial anger from his parents, they eventually accepted his choice. His father now decorates his offices with Jamal's artwork.

Now it's your turn to highlight some of the messages you received from the significant people in your early life regarding creativity. By doing this exercise you'll have the opportunity to throw some light on what might be getting in the way of embracing your creative life. You'll also have the opportunity to 're-write' these messages into what you need to hear now in order to move forward. Firstly, let's have a look at what Jamal remembered and wrote in his journal.

Significant person	Messages they gave me
From Dad	Art is a waste of time.
	Art is for sissies.
	You must make good money in order to be successful.
From Mum	Real men don't draw and paint. You should be like your father. Get a real job to provide for a future family.

Significant person	Messages they gave me
Mrs Klaasen (Year 9 Art Teacher)	You have something special. Your ideas are so imaginative. Great skills.
What messages can I give myself now?	I love painting and it's okay for me to do it now. I'll remember what Mrs Klaasen used to say.

Before you begin, it's worth pointing out that the messages we remember may not be as overt and/or deliberately negative as the ones Jamal received. Sometimes children interpret 'grown-up' behaviour and what is said in a way that is not intended. Penny, a friend of mine in art class, gained a helpful insight the other day after struggling to paint more expressively. She remembered how her loving mum would often say, 'You are such a good, tidy girl, Penny.' She liked being 'tidy' in all sorts of ways, but this did not fit with wanting to have a looser, experimental approach to her painting. Once she realised she didn't have to follow this 'old' message from her mother, she became a lot freer. Now it's your turn to think about some of the messages you received.

DISCOVERING MESSAGES FROM THE PAST

Part 1: As you were growing up who were the significant people in your life — parents, siblings, school teachers, friends, etc? Write down their names on one side of a page in your journal. If you don't remember a name, write down their role, such as 'teacher'.

What were the messages they gave you about creativity? These messages may have been positive or negative; things people said out loud or even just suggested; messages about creativity in general, or your own or other people's creativity. Write down the messages opposite their name.

Part 2: Now take a look at these messages. Do you still believe them? Are they helpful or unhelpful? If unhelpful, what do you think would be more helpful or encouraging messages? Are you willing to start giving yourself these messages?

Note: If you find it difficult to think of encouraging messages, you are not alone. This is something that for many people takes practice. Later chapters will show you how. So for now, just keep writing. As in any area of our lives, it's okay to just have a go even if you are not entirely sure of what to do. I know many times I have felt uncertain as I put paint to canvas only to later repaint what I've done.

SELF-COMPASSION

This chapter has encouraged you to explore past influences and this can sometimes stir up different feelings and thoughts. Maybe you discovered painful memories or powerful early messages that have impacted on how you view yourself or your attitudes towards creativity. I hope you also recollected enjoyable scenes. However, if difficult or unpleasant memories emerged, self-compassion is a powerful way to heal old wounds. Self-compassion is also a much-needed companion as you continue on your creative journey.

Self-compassion is a way of being kind and caring towards

yourself. Think about how you feel when someone you care about is upset. Perhaps they feel sad or hurt or maybe they feel inadequate or self-critical because they have made a mistake. Hopefully, as a friend, you notice how they feel rather than dismissing or judging them. You are kind and you show you care by listening and saying something supportive. You don't criticise and tell them what they *should* do, although a little later you might make a helpful suggestion. This feeling of compassion includes understanding that suffering and imperfection are both part of being human. We are all influenced to some degree by our past and present life circumstances. We all suffer sometimes.

You might find the notion of compassion quite new and challenging. Perhaps you wonder whether you have the capacity to be compassionate towards a friend the way I just described. That's okay. Give yourself time to understand the nature of compassion.

Self-compassion is about learning how to be your own best friend. It's not about self-pity, which is feeling sorry for yourself and keeping yourself in a helpless state by thinking, 'I feel so awful. There's nothing I can do.' Self-compassion is about recognising the reality, even if something you have done seems like a mistake. You might even see the humour. When you are self-compassionate, you acknowledge your feelings and think of ways to be kind to yourself. For example, phoning a friend or having a long, hot soak in a bath.

In this book I'll continue to encourage self-compassion, especially when dealing with the struggles of creativity. In Chapter Twelve, I'll discuss mindfulness, a practice that helps you to become more self-compassionate. In future chapters you'll continue to have opportunities to understand yourself better. Self-compassion needs to be at the forefront of this discovery, so come back to the above explanation whenever you need a reminder.

CREATIVE TOUCHSTONES

I wonder what you discovered in this chapter? Did the exercises help you to recognise how life events and historical influences have impacted on how you experience your own creativity? Hopefully you found some positive memories, but maybe some painful memories emerged. Cultivating compassion can help you to deal with the common challenges we all face from time to time when we create. When you are able to nourish and respect your creativity, particularly if it has been ignored or denied in the past, you have the opportunity for profound self-growth and healing.

Chapter Four

THE CREATIVE SEED

Creative activity could be described as a type of learning process where teacher and pupil are located in the same individual.

— ARTHUR KOESTLER

This chapter explores both the nature of a creative person and the process of learning and developing your creative expression. You'll discover that creativity isn't something mysterious and beyond your grasp. On the contrary, by breaking down the creative process into stages, you can take yourself on a journey that is satisfying and fascinating. The creative seed will grow. I particularly like the seed imagery as it neatly encapsulates the **S**kills, **E**xperimentation, **E**valuation and **D**iscovery that occur in all creative paths — the SEED.

THE CHARACTERISTICS OF CREATIVE PEOPLE

Creative people come from all walks of life. They can be poor, rich, educated or uneducated. Research has found, however, that there are common characteristics shared by creative people such as persistence, courage, curiosity and playfulness. People who create develop a fascination for what they do and learn how to solve the inevitable problems or challenges that come their way. They learn to tolerate the highs and lows of the creative process — to be flexible and play with ideas, especially unusual ones. Can you remember an occasion when you were persistent? Curious? Courageous? Flexible? Played with ideas? I suspect you can remember at least one, but if you are finding it difficult, don't despair. As you continue to read this book you will find lots of strategies to encourage these ways of being.

WHAT DOES CREATIVITY INVOLVE?

Creativity involves our senses of seeing, hearing, smelling, touching and being intuitive. It also involves different ways of thinking such as comparing, evaluating, asking interesting questions and problem solving. Our creativity is not only active when we are engaged in our creative expression, but can be constantly stimulated as we go about our everyday lives. I love to paint and I'm continually engaged in the creative process as I observe and find myself fascinated by colours, shapes, lighting, pictures in books and what I see in art galleries. My fascination was only modest at the start but it has grown over the years. My partner, a writer, is intrigued by words and phrases he hears in everyday conversations or reads anywhere. His creative-self continues to be stimulated away from the writing desk. Whatever your interest or passion, your mind takes in cues from all around you. The key is to be 'engaged' in your creative expression by giving it regular time and energy.

So is there a certain way we go about being creative regardless of our particular interest or discipline? Do writers, songwriters, art and craft makers travel the same journey? Well, yes, they do! Many people believe creativity is something you achieve. For example, something is made — a painting, a sculpture or a quilt. Or something is performed — a character in a play, a song or a piece of music. Usually people believe that what is *produced* is creative; however, while we appreciate and enjoy what we see or hear, it is what *happens* 'behind the scenes' that is really what creativity is about. For example, drawing lots of sketches to work out your landscape composition, going over and over a piece of music, or experimenting in getting the right voice for a character in your novel — these are the times when you are practising or experimenting and working out what you want to express. This is creativity.

TWO STEPS DIVIDED INTO FOUR

The first step in the creative process is to give yourself permission to start — to be a beginner. We need to learn some of the basic techniques and gain some experience. This permission seems obvious, I know, but as we discovered in previous chapters, some people believe they are not creative. They don't give themselves the opportunity to learn or to play with some of the foundational techniques of their art or craft (drawing, woodturning, sculpting, etc.). Or to gain some experience in an area they love, such as acting, singing or writing. Remember my story of drawing an awkward misshapen jug? A crude beginning, but it was an essential start. If I had walked away from that first attempt I would have missed discovering something that has added such colour and pleasure to my life.

The second main step is a willingness to take risks and experiment with the skills and the knowledge that you accumulate. This takes time, practice and playfulness. In fact, this second step continues forever and is where your own stamp on creativity develops.

The SEED concept opens up these two steps into four main areas that are part of the creative process:

S – Skills

E – Experimentation

E – Evaluation

D – Discovery.

Skills

So what is the first step for you? Do you need to:

- Draw simple shapes?
- Audition for a local play?
- Buy some sculpting clay?
- Write a poem?
- Attend an art class?
- Learn how to crochet or knit?
- Join a writers' group?
- Sing in the shower?
- Learn how to mix paints?
- Learn how to use a lathe?
- Attend concerts/art exhibitions/the theatre?
- Build a box?
- Arrange an unusual flower display?
- Read a play out loud?
- Shape a tree?
- Play some notes or short tunes on a piano, guitar or recorder?

We all need to learn some techniques and gain experience. This means practising and building on what you already know. It is also about playfulness — playing with your pencils, paints, words on a page, phrasing of a song or a piece of music. Appreciate all these early steps and see them as necessary for your creative growth.

Creative connection

Developing skills includes being curious about and fascinated by your area of interest. Writers read other people's books for inspiration and they are fascinated by life. Painters are inspired by what they see in their environment and other people's art. Singers are captivated by melody and listen with curiosity to hear how other singers arrange and interpret songs. This is how we all learn. We start to make connections to what we already know and then use our imagination to build on these connections. If you are a musician you may know some basic guitar chords and then you hear something more sophisticated by another musician. At first you connect this to what you already know and then see if you can play a more complex piece of music. You are building one skill on another. Crocheting skills provide a valuable foundation for extending your craft into lace making.

Some of you already have many techniques and skills you have accumulated over time and therefore need to challenge yourself to keep practising, experimenting and extending your repertoire and experience.

Creative cross-fertilisation

Perhaps you already have skills in a particular creative domain, but you want to try your hand at something different. Maybe you are a musician, or simply love music, but also want to develop your painting skills. You will find that one area of creativity stimulates another. You can ask yourself, 'What does this music invoke in me? What colours/shapes/words come to mind as I listen? What's the mood of this music and how might this translate to painting?' Your love of music can activate a whole host of creative ideas for a new fascination in painting.

No matter what area of creativity you are already enjoying, you can find inspiration to influence your approach in a brand new area. I find that my understanding of colour theory, which I learnt about in art class, has helped me in experimenting with colour and texture in creative knitting. It's exciting to reap the benefits of this creative cross-fertilisation.

The value of imitation

It's fine to imitate as you learn new skills. That's how we first learn. Photographers look at other people's photography and, if they like certain effects, try to do the same. Writers might try writing a short story in the vein of Ernest Hemingway. Painters often have lessons and at first imitate their teachers or other artists. Dancers learn steps and movements from teachers then progress to creating new movements and combining old movements in new ways. Imitation and repetition in expressing your art is legitimate and valuable. Paul McCartney, when interviewed by Ken Robinson, said that at the start of his music career he copied and pretended to be Little Richard and Elvis, while John Lennon imitated Jerry Lee Lewis and Chuck Berry!

Creativity and re-creativity

Some creativity is re-creativity — think of the number of interpretations of the song 'Summertime'. Singers need to harness their own inventiveness to convey something unique to the audience. Similarly, musicians frequently play music that has been interpreted by many others. They need to find their own connection to the music in order to engage the audience. Jazz musicians in particular are skilled at improvisation or creating a new take on a piece of music or song. Artists are often drawn to landscapes that have been painted before. However, each artist expresses and interprets what they see.

SKILL BUILDING

In your journal write about the skills or experience you already have.
- *What techniques have you learnt so far?*
- *What do you need or want to learn next?*
- *What can you begin to do in order to learn these skills?*

Experimentation

The second step in the SEED process is experimentation. Being creative is in the *doing*. It's important to give yourself regular time to express and experiment in your particular creative domain. This takes commitment.

When we experiment we keep our mind open to new ideas, new problems and challenges and how to go about solving them. So test out your ideas and see what happens when you try something different. Ask yourself lots of questions. 'Do I want to develop this further?', 'What happens if I do it this way?' and 'What could I try out next?' are good ones to keep in mind. Be willing to play with your art material, words on a page, sounds from your voice/instrument, clay, wood or whatever material you are using. Be willing to improvise and experiment without having a goal in mind except the drive to 'see what happens'. Let yourself have fun. Being too serious can take away the joy and this ultimately demotivates you. We learn from what we *don't* like as much as from what we *do* like. You don't have to do this on your own. You can take classes. You can read books. You might have friends with whom you can creatively play. Check out what's available in your community. There might be writers' centres, art courses, music and singing tuition and different craft groups. Your library noticeboard can be an excellent place to see what's available in your local area. And of course there is always the Internet, where you will find many resources.

EXPERIMENTING WITH EXPERIMENTATION

In your journal brainstorm some ways you can experiment within your creative domain. Are there unusual ways you can express yourself just for the experience of trying something different? No one needs to see or hear what you do. This is just for you. See what happens when you take some risks.

Evaluation

There is a fine line between constructively evaluating and being overly critical about your creativity. If you are a beginner, I suggest you focus on the first two stages of the SEED process — that is, building skills and experimenting playfully. However, if you are further along your creative path you also need to evaluate what you do, to ask yourself: 'What do I like about what I am doing? What do I want to change?'

You can devise a whole series of questions to help you evaluate your work. These questions will depend on your particular interest or discipline but here are a few examples to get you started.

If you are a fiction writer:
Is this character's voice consistent?
Is there sufficient continuity in my chapters?
Do I need light and shade? Humour?

If you are a painter:
Where is the focal point?
What do I want to convey?
Is there sufficient tonality?

If you are a singer:
What part of my life or me does this song connect to?
Is this the best key for me?
What emotion do I want to convey?

If you are a dancer:
What do I want the audience to feel?
Is the storyline clear?
Have I got sufficient feedback from the others in my group?

If you are a potter:
Is this decorative pattern too busy?
Do I need to reglaze this pot?
Is this a functional piece or for display only?

Spontaneity

There are many myths surrounding famous creative people to suggest their genius is purely instinctive and without experimentation and evaluation. For example, it has been said the English Romantic poets Coleridge and Blake were spontaneous in their writing. However, significant evidence has been found to the contrary. The poets' own notebooks show they spent time writing down their ideas, evaluating and revising what they had written.

Discovery

Discovery is all about finding our own unique approach to creativity. It happens each time we create and develops over time from an increasing and intimate understanding of our creative discipline. We unearth an approach to our creativity that is distinctive, innovative and original. We find our own style. This style can change many times or it can become the 'trademark' of how we create.

An excellent example of innovation and originality is Picasso's painting 'Les Demoiselles d'Avignon' painted in 1907. This painting has been called the most important painting of the last century because it is seen as a dramatic shift away from the artistic conventions of that time. To many it was seen as pure genius. However, 'Les Demoiselles', although innovative, didn't come out of the blue. The painting has similarities to what Picasso had done before as well as to other artists' work at that time. Historians found Picasso's sketches of the painting and know that he visited brothels and hospitals to do his research. His genius lay in his willingness to experiment and combine many ideas to produce something original. This was his discovery and it was a process that took time.

So, if you are a beginner, don't put pressure on yourself to be innovative. Allow it to unfold. This often occurs after you have built up your skills and experience. As your creative seed begins to grow, watch out for what seems to touch you personally, and give this time and attention. This may be the stirring of your unique creative gift.

THE CREATIVE LOOP

We all start somewhere. We begin with a desire to try something new, perhaps we have a few techniques or some experience. We practise, play and experiment. Even with just a few skills we can start to be innovative, but as we grow in confidence we build a rich foundation to extend our creativity and give our own flavour to the painting, the song, the tune, the character or the writing. This is where originality flourishes — but it takes persistence! Again, don't put pressure on yourself to be innovative and original at the start. Originality takes time, sometimes years. The important thing is to begin with those early steps. You will grow in the ability to be creative. I promise!

As you can see in the diagram on the next page, the SEED process is not something that you do in sequential stages but rather it is a process that continually turns back on itself time and again as we engage in creative expression. We experience SEED growth in a creative session, over many sessions and within our creative lifetime. And as the creative spiral shows, there is an ever-growing expansion of our skills, experimentation and our ability to ask innovative questions and be original.

CREATIVE TOUCHSTONES

Creativity is an ever-evolving loop of learning skills, experimenting, evaluating and bringing forth something unique from you, the creator, in whatever field you choose. There is continuous movement back and forth that expands into greater knowledge as you move along this loop.

Although there are common characteristics shared by creative people, playfulness and persistence are key elements in keeping the creative seed alive, whether you are a beginner or well established.

You are now ready for Part Two of this book. This section addresses common obstacles all creative people experience. It also provides well-respected and tested techniques and strategies that I hope will inspire you to find productive ways to achieve your goals.

PART TWO

GUIDING YOUR CREATIVE-SELF

Chapter Five

SELF-TALK AND CREATIVITY

*You are your own friend and
you are your own enemy.*

— FROM THE BHAGAVAD GITA

Are you aware of the conversations you have inside your head? The inner voice that comments, interprets and judges? What we think can either help or hinder our progress in creative expression. As you read and do the exercises in this chapter you'll have the opportunity to discover your own thought patterns, see their effect on your behaviour and observe how self-talk can either thwart or encourage your creative progress. You will have the opportunity to develop strategies that guide and support you. If this is your first introduction to self-talk, give yourself time to complete the exercises and come back to them several times. For many it takes courage to really listen to what goes on inside the mind, but it is the start of freeing yourself and releasing your creative spirit.

WHAT IS SELF-TALK?

For many years we have known from psychological research and practical experience that it's not always the particular situation that creates stress or discomfort but how we *think* about the situation. Of course, we think about lots of things from the mundane to the complex. We plan, reflect and respond to what's going on in our day and the world around us. But our mind also chatters about other things, including thoughts about our own worth and capability. Our inner voice often seems automatic and we believe we have little control over it. Let me tell you about Geoff.

GEOFF

Geoff is eighteen years old. He has just left school and he is taking a year off to earn some money to support himself through university. He wants to study journalism. He loves to write short stories and has ideas for a first novel. Often when he sits down to write he feels discouraged because it seems to take such a long time for the words to flow. Let's listen to Geoff's inner voice as he sits down to write: 'Here I go again, this is so painful, like pulling teeth. Who will want to ever read my stuff anyway? I can't stand this — I'll go and have a cup of coffee.'

Geoff's self-talk is reflecting an underlying belief that he isn't good enough. This is a common belief and we will have individual ways of talking to ourselves in order to hammer it in even further.

What is encouraging is that we *can* find more helpful ways to think that will support what we want to do.

TUNE IN

The first step to changing your self-talk is *heightening your awareness* of your inner voice. At first some people have difficulty recognising that it's even there. If this is the case for you, that's okay. Give yourself time to listen carefully to what's going on inside your mind. Sometimes your inner voice is quiet and insidious, but unfortunately that can be just as potent as someone else's inner voice that is 'loud'. So, to begin with, tune in to what's happening inside. Be a curious observer. Take a piece of paper or a small notebook with you as you go about your day and from time to time take a moment to write down what your mind is telling you about yourself and what's happening around you. Perhaps as you sit on the bus or take the dog for a walk, notice and become aware of your inner chatter.

STUMBLING BLOCKS

There are a few different thought patterns that can cause us to stumble and obstruct our creative progress. The first relates to the thoughts we have about our own competence, what we believe others think and our attitude towards the creative task. The next exercise asks you to write down your thoughts or self-talk at a time when you want to create but feel discouraged in some way — perhaps anxious or reluctant. For now this is an observation exercise, but it will be followed by a well-respected strategy to manage your self-talk.

SELF-TALK AND THE CREATIVE TASK

*In your journal, write down your thoughts and feelings
as you approach your creative time. What do you say to
yourself? How do you feel when you think this way? Do you
continue to do the creative task you set out to do? If so, how
do you feel and how does it go? Be aware of your self-talk as
you continue. Observe how you feel and what you experience
in your body. For example, do you feel tense in your
shoulders, neck or anywhere else? Does your stomach churn?
What do you do? Do you continue or do you walk away
from what you are doing? If something like this happens
try to have an attitude of compassion towards yourself. No
judgment — just gentle observation. Now is a good time to re-
read the section on self-compassion in Chapter Three.*

The next step is learning how to evaluate your self-talk: to work
out if it's actually true and whether it's helpful. *Just because you
think it, doesn't make it accurate.* I highlighted that sentence
because it's so important and needs to be carefully considered
and taken in. We usually believe everything we tell ourselves, but
there are times when what we tell ourselves is negative, untrue
or exaggerated. First of all let's see what Stefano, a songwriter,
says inside his head and then we'll find out how he challenges
his unhelpful self-talk.

STEFANO

Stefano is about to sit down and work out some lyrics
for a piece of music he has written.

Stefano thinks

About self: 'I can't do this — my words will sound stupid.'

About others: 'They think I'm pretentious anyway.'

About the task: 'It's so hard to make a start.'

I am sure you can see how this self-talk discourages Stefano. What can he do? In order for him to move forward he needs to ask himself two important questions:

- Is each thought true or untrue?
- Is each thought helpful or unhelpful?

Let's see how he puts this into practice.

1. Is each thought true or untrue?

Stefano needs to challenge and dispute the three aspects of his thinking. He asks himself, 'Where's the evidence this thought is accurate?' This is how he answers:

About self: I can't do this – my words will sound stupid. 'Well, there is no evidence this thought is true. I have written lyrics before. No one has ever said they are stupid.'

About others: They think I'm pretentious anyway. 'No one, other than my brother, has ever inferred that it might be a waste of time. And he was commenting on the money side only.'

About the task: It's so hard to make a start. 'It's difficult to start when I'm thinking of all the negatives. I need to remember it doesn't have to be perfect.'

2. Is each thought helpful or unhelpful?

By seeing his thoughts written down Stefano sees how unhelpful they are. He writes: 'The thoughts, once looked at, aren't even true. If I think this way I feel lousy — it doesn't get me anywhere. I feel like running away.'

As you can see, Stefano needs to step back from his self-talk rather than get absorbed in it. When he gives himself time to challenge his inner voice and replace it with realistic and helpful self-talk, he is ready to start experimenting with ideas for his lyrics.

Now it's your turn. You can either return to the occasion you used for the previous exercise or you can choose another time when you engaged in your creativity and had some difficulty.

CHALLENGE YOUR OWN THINKING

Ask yourself the following questions and challenge your own thinking. You can then find self-talk that is realistic and helpful.

- *What is the creative task?*
- *What do I think?*
  - *about myself?*
  - *about others?*
  - *about the task?*
- *How do I feel when I think this way?*

For each thought answer these questions:

1. *Is this thought true? Is it 100 per cent accurate? Identify times when it has not been true. Could it be just my interpretation? Am I exaggerating? What is a more*

realistic thought? What's another way I could look at this?

2. *Is this thought helpful? If I didn't believe this thought, how would things be different? What's a more helpful way of seeing this?*

By doing this exercise I hope you are discovering that what you say to yourself is linked to how you feel and what you do. You are also learning how to challenge your unhelpful thinking and replace it with support and encouragement. When you start doing things differently you might feel a bit weird, but don't let this stop you. Keep going — as time goes on you will find it easier to be vigilant towards unhelpful self-talk and changing it to be encouraging. We *can* learn to be like this with ourselves. It's similar to how we would boost a good friend, colleague or a child who needs some encouragement. If you can do it for them, you can do it for yourself. This is what I call our Inner Supporter and I will tell you more about this aspect of yourself in the next chapter.

OTHER STUMBLING BLOCKS

Let's go a bit further now and see how just a few negative thoughts can lead to a cascade of other stumbling blocks to creativity. Let me tell you about Kate.

KATE

Kate loved photography when she was a teenager, but for many years she was busy bringing up a family and working part time. Now that the children are older she wants to take some photos of nature, just as she loved doing many years before. She is excited and buys herself her first digital camera. At first she is enthusiastic and takes lots of pictures but she is disappointed with the results. She is hard on herself. She remembers the criticism she used to get from her mother and from a particular teacher when she was about fourteen years old. She sets out again to take more photos and finds herself feeling uncomfortable and anxious. She notices a voice in her head saying she is hopeless and that it is too late to even try.

Let's have a look at what's happening to Kate. You'll see that her self-talk is similar to that of Geoff and Stefano in the earlier examples. However, there are additional ways her mind trips her up. One stumbling block leads on to the next.

KATE'S STUMBLING BLOCKS

Self-talk:

About self: 'Who do I think I am? I'm hopeless at this. It's too late for me.'

About others: 'I'm sure Pete thinks I'm ridiculous getting back into this. My sister always said I was airy-fairy. Wait till she finds out.'

About the task: 'It's so difficult — I always struggle with it. These photos are terrible!'

Painful memories:

Teacher ridiculing her work.

Mother being critical when she showed her her Visual Arts project in Year 8.

Sister teasing her.

Discouraging fantasies:

'The same thing will happen next time I take shots so why bother?'

'Life will continue to be work, work and more work with no time for fun.'

These stumbling blocks lead to:

Feeling tired, anxious and discouraged.

A sense of failure.

Resulting behaviour:

Puts off taking more photos.

Snappy and irritable towards her family.

Stress-related physical symptoms:

Tension headaches.

Upset stomach.

As you can see there's not just one stumbling block on Kate's creative path. She has several and they topple into each other, compounding their impact on her self-confidence. She has unhelpful thoughts about her competence and what others think of her. She switches into exaggerating and catastrophising and believing her photography is 'awful' and that it's all just a huge 'struggle'. She tells herself that she won't succeed in achieving what she wants. This triggers memories from the past and understandably Kate ends up feeling tense and unhappy. Her mood has changed from one of excitement to feeling down and irritable. This discourages her from having another go. Not only does she feel unhappy but she is affected physically and is irritable with her family. Can you see how just a few thoughts can gather momentum?

GUIDEPOSTS

The good news is that Kate can begin to move any one of her stumbling blocks and this will make her creative journey easier to navigate. *'She can start by learning ways to deal with her unhelpful thoughts just as Stefano did. Or she can learn some relaxation strategies to help with the physical tension she experiences in her body. Or she can keep taking photos and not give in to her despondency. Any one of these three options will help.'* Let's look at the ideal. If she addressed each of the above areas by placing helpful guideposts, her creative path might look something like this:

Kate's guideposts on her creative path

Self-talk:

About self: 'I have a real passion to take great photos. I might be a little rusty, but I will get better. I'm forty and I have many years left to do what I love.'

About others: 'I know Pete is encouraging and so are my friends Don and Louise. I can let go of what my sister thinks. I'm a grown-up now and she can't really hurt me.'

About the task: 'It's new for me again — I'll have an experimental approach and have fun with it.'

Encouraging memories:
Receiving an art prize in Year 10.
A photo gaining recognition in a local competition.

Encouraging fantasies:
Sees herself out in the country enjoying taking photos.
Sees herself in a year's time with an impressive portfolio.

These guideposts lead to:
Feeling excited.

Resulting behaviour:
Experiments with different ways of taking photos.
Goes into the bush for two hours.
Joins a night class on photography.

Physical response:
Fewer tension headaches and uses relaxation techniques to calm herself when anxious.

It looks encouraging, doesn't it? I'm not suggesting that the only way you will be creative is to switch on all of the above, permanently. It's not a static, definite mindset or set of behaviours that you must have in order to enjoy and grow creatively. I hope though that the above example gives you a picture of what is a helpful way to approach your creative activities. Remember that you can work on one stumbling block at a time and introduce one guidepost at a time. This chapter specifically targets our thinking patterns, or self-talk, while further chapters focus on other aspects of the creative path, such as managing stress, setting goals and dealing with procrastination.

WHAT ABOUT YOU?

I wonder whether, in reading Kate's story, you recognised one or two stumbling blocks that trip you up? Many of us think this way some of the time. We need to become our own best detective and discover what we do inside our minds. Curiosity and an attitude of non-judgment and self-compassion are needed for this investigation!

THE ROLE OF MEMORIES

Let's go back to Kate's stumbling blocks about her photography. She not only had negative thoughts about herself, the task and what she believed others were thinking, but she also recalled memories that were discouraging — particularly criticism from others. One thought reinforced the next.

When feeling down or discouraged, the mind is like a magnet attracting more 'proof' that your thinking is accurate. These memories serve to reinforce the other stumbling blocks. However, as you saw in Kate's example, she also had memories that were positive. So rather than focusing on the negative memories, it's much more inspiring to deliberately bring out positive ones. This dampens down the negative memories. So

I encourage you to dig deep, either in the distant past or not so distant past, and find times that are more encouraging to think about. But first of all let me tell you about filtering.

Filtering

Why do we seem to be so good at remembering negative memories? Well, unconsciously we are supporting some underlying beliefs about ourselves. It is what makes us feel 'right' about ourselves, even though we might feel miserable when we get engulfed in these thoughts and memories. If your underlying belief is that you are not good enough/smart enough/ creative enough, you tend to view the world and yourself in ways that reinforce this belief. Unconsciously you may filter out or dismiss encouraging and helpful messages that go against your belief system while easily absorbing and letting in messages that reinforce it. Here are two examples:

A teacher says to Mel: 'Why don't you add more colour?' Her automatic thought is: 'Yep, I knew it. It's terrible.'

A friend says, 'That's a great piece of work!' but Mel thinks, 'She's only saying that to be nice.'

See how Mel filters out the positives? She now has another negative memory to recall that reinforces her belief that she isn't good enough.

Just as you are learning to challenge your unhelpful self-talk, you can also learn to take in the encouragement you are starting to give yourself and that you hear from others. Learning how to accept the positives takes practice because initially it feels like going against the grain.

The next exercise asks you to search carefully and to bring

into your awareness a number of positive experiences to put into your memory bag. They do not need to be about your particular creative interest. These memories can come from any area of your life.

MY RESERVOIR OF ENCOURAGING MEMORIES

1. In your journal, write down positive and encouraging things people have said to you about any area of your life. Give thought to whether you have filtered or dismissed things people have said.

2. Write or draw about an area of your life (past or present) when you felt/feel:
- *happy*
- *competent*
- *relaxed*
- *playful*
- *organised*
- *spontaneous.*

3. And now revisit your area of creative activity. Think of as many encouraging memories as you can — a pat on the back, an encouraging word or praise, your own joy or satisfaction. You made a start on this in Chapter Three, but keep going with it. You may find that there are many more in storage from the past and others from recent experiences — perhaps some that you previously filtered or dismissed.

You can remind yourself of these positive memories in the following ways:

- *Write them on special cards that you can pull out and read anytime, particularly if you are feeling discouraged.*
- *Write them in pop-up boxes on your computer.*
- *Enjoy sharing your memories with others.*
- *Express your memories creatively: write a poem/song/story, draw/paint or express your memories in dance or music.*

UNREALISTIC FANTASIES

Future-oriented fantasies have a similar impact to memories and can be unrealistically positive or negative. Negative fantasies influence us in the same way that unhelpful self-talk or memories do. Remember how Kate, the photographer, said, 'The same thing will happen next time I take shots so why bother?' Well, I'm sure you can see why this sort of fantasy would be discouraging. What's a more helpful and realistic alternative for Kate? Perhaps something like: 'I'll have another go. I learnt a lot from taking this first batch of photos. I'll keep going and take some better ones.' Not only is that much more encouraging, but it's also both honest and realistic.

Sometimes positive fantasies can be just as unhelpful as negative ones. We explored in Chapter One the value of dreams, wishes and fantasies. They can be an inspiration to help us move forward on our journey. (This long-term vision is about yourself and the goals that are important to you and how you are going to get there, and we'll explore it in detail in Chapter Eight.) However, sometimes people have unrealistic fantasies that are not about what they will do to achieve their fantasy but about others and society giving them what they think they deserve. For example, a reclusive writer might fantasise about finally being discovered and becoming rich and famous. This is not realistic unless part of the fantasy is also about getting out and taking the necessary steps to get his book published. And even then, such a specific fantasy of becoming rich and famous needs to be realistically examined.

FANTASIES

In your journal write down any fantasies you have about your creative pursuit. Do they include what you will do on the way to making this fantasy come true, or are they centred on discovery by others and the 'magic' of unrealism?

In the next chapter you will continue to fine-tune your skills in managing your self-talk by understanding different aspects of your personality.

CREATIVE TOUCHSTONES

This chapter has encouraged you to be aware of your thinking patterns, or self-talk, and how these impact on your creative time. Through reading this chapter and the stories of others I hope you have discovered:

- unhelpful ways of thinking that thwart your journey
- helpful and realistic ways of thinking that inspire you to move ahead and do what you love
- the impact of fantasies and memories and how they influence your creative time.

Chapter Six

THE DEFLATING DUO BEHIND CREATIVITY

Every person has certain qualities or presences in their heart which are awkward, disturbing and negative. One of your sacred duties is to exercise kindness towards them.

— JOHN O'DONOHUE

In this chapter you'll have the opportunity to discover and practise strategies to manage two potent parts of your personality: the Inner Critic and the Inner Softie. These are the deflating duo of creative life. You are likely to be nodding your head in understanding when you hear the term Inner Critic, but you may well be somewhat bemused by the term Inner Softie. Wait and see! I'm sure by the end of the chapter many of you will recognise this part of your personality and understand how it gets in the way of your creative expression. You will also have the opportunity to develop two dynamic allies for your creative life: the Inner Supporter and the Inner Guide. While the Critic and Softie deflate, the Supporter and Guide boost, inspire and take you forward.

THE INNER CRITIC

As we discovered in the last chapter, managing your inner voice is a powerful way to free yourself from constraints so that you can develop your creative expression. You learnt how to challenge and evaluate your negative self-talk and found ways to give yourself realistic and helpful messages. However, sometimes negative self-talk takes a lot to manage, especially when it's highly critical and harsh. We'll call this part of ourselves the Inner Critic.

Let's have a look at the different ways the Inner Critic can manifest in our lives and in particular with regards to our creativity. The Inner Critic might shoot us down with nasty *labels*: 'I'm a hopeless drawer' or 'My take on that song is so boring.' The Inner Critic might criticise our *behaviour*: 'I made so many stupid mistakes in my music practice' or 'I stuffed up that line — the scene flopped.' The Inner Critic can be very heavy handed with *shoulds* and *musts*: 'You should always finish one project before starting another' or 'You must sculpt this way.' The Inner Critic uses extreme words such as *always* and *never*: 'I always get it wrong' or 'I'll never get anywhere with this.' Our Inner Critic is also well practised at *comparing* us with other people. Someone is always smarter, more talented, draws better, writes better, sings better, than us.

Where does the Inner Critic come from?

The Inner Critic reflects how we have internalised moral and authoritative messages from significant people in our past, particularly our parents but also grandparents, teachers, peer groups, religious and other influential institutions. We weren't born with an Inner Critic but very early in life started hearing or even sensing what we *should* and *should not* do, what was *good* behaviour and what was *bad*. We learnt quickly and before long we started to give ourselves similar messages. Some of these messages are helpful. Parents say things like, 'Be careful when you cross a busy road!' or 'Don't talk with your mouth full of food.' Naturally we need to keep telling ourselves these sorts of messages in order to function well. But there may have been other messages that dampened our spirit and self-esteem. Critical messages such as 'Don't be so stupid!' or 'Get out of my way!' that diminished our worth as a person. There may have been messages that attacked our behaviour and ability to do things: 'You can't do anything right' or 'You're hopeless.' These examples might not be the exact words: there are endless variations, mild or severe, and you may well have your own examples to draw from. They don't even have to be verbal messages. Looks of disapproval, aggression and any form of abuse can lead us to feeling that we are not worthy or capable. We pick up these messages early on in childhood, during our teenage years and even in later life when we are vulnerable. Sometimes we continue to give ourselves these messages in a variety of ways, as we explored in the previous section. These are the nasty labels, the attacks on our behaviour, the 'shoulds', 'musts', 'always' and 'nevers', and unflattering comparisons to other people.

Unmasking your Inner Critic

You might very easily identify with having an active Inner Critic or perhaps only a little. But regardless of how much you identify with this part of your personality, increasing your awareness of this aspect of yourself can be liberating. It's like clearing out your wardrobe — it helps you to find out what's in there and decide what to keep and what to let go of. The following exercise asks you to externalise your Inner Critic: to transform what is on the inside to the outside. It's important to see the Inner Critic for what it is and what it says, rather than leave it furtively eroding your self-confidence. So let's get it out!

YOUR INNER CRITIC

Find a large sheet of paper or use your journal and draw or paint your Inner Critic. This is not an artistic exercise, so it doesn't matter how it's done. You might want to draw something specific, like a character, or do something abstract and draw all sorts of shapes and sizes or sharp lines to depict your Inner Critic. Surround your picture with some of the negative messages this part of you tells you. These may be words, phrases, 'shoulds' or some of the other derogatory ways of giving messages that I mentioned earlier.

How did you go? After doing this exercise be careful not to judge yourself harshly by saying something like, 'I'm so stupid doing this to myself.' This, of course, would be your Inner Critic emerging again. Just see the Inner Critic as an inner voice that's not helpful and needs taming.

Disarming your Inner Critic

As you can see, the Inner Critic is negative, picky and discouraging, so why does it hang around so much? Why don't we just get rid of it? Perhaps you have tried and it hasn't worked.

First of all the Inner Critic needs to be understood. We need to discover its purpose. There are different reasons that are usually unconscious, so let's see if we can bring them into awareness. Once you do, it's much easier to deal with the Inner Critic.

Your Inner Critic might be trying to protect you in some way: 'If I put you down, I'll stop you from going ahead and making a fool of yourself' or 'If I put you down you won't have far to fall.'

The Inner Critic might be well meaning in trying to whip you into shape or success: 'Get on with it, you lazy thing.' It thinks that by criticising you, you will get things done. Well perhaps you will, but often at the expense of your self-esteem. And typically after obeying our Inner Critic for a while, we stop and give up because we never really please it. If you have ever gone on a diet you will know what I mean. This is where the Inner Critic pushes you into being 'good' and careful with food, but to such an extent that eventually you rebel and eat whatever you want.

The Inner Critic might be trying to desensitise you to criticism you fear from others. Underneath, you believe that if you criticise yourself then it won't be so awful when others do it. You might say to a friend, 'This is a terrible sculpture. I'm such an amateur!' because this is what you think your friend thinks! You want to get in first.

The Inner Critic has a fatalistic and bleak outlook on life. It doesn't see the exciting possibilities waiting for you as you move into supporting and encouraging your creativity. The next exercise helps to uncover the intention of your Inner Critic.

DIALOGUE WITH THE INNER CRITIC

Imagine your Inner Critic as a separate part of yourself, so you can have a conversation and find out a bit more about it. You can place the drawing or painting you did in the previous exercise in front of you to help you to see your Inner Critic as a separate entity. Writing in your journal, ask your Inner Critic the following questions and see what it answers.

- *What are you telling me?*
- *Why do you keep telling me these things?*
- *What are you hoping to do by telling me all these things?*

Feel free to answer back and continue the dialogue. Sometimes the dialogue comes easily and sometimes it takes time.

Do you understand your Inner Critic a little better now? As with some of the other exercises, you may need to mull over this information and allow your thoughts to evolve. Often when we are introduced to a new idea, we need time to think about it and let it sink in. Let's do some further work with your Inner Critic.

Deflating your Inner Critic

There are different ways to manage your Inner Critic so that it's not so powerful in dampening your creative spirit and perhaps even stopping you from doing what you want to do. Besides evaluating its accuracy and helpfulness and replacing it with encouraging and helpful self-talk, as we did in the last chapter, here are some other ideas:

- Create a ritual with your drawing or painting of the Inner Critic: burn it, tear it up into little pieces or fold it up tightly and put it in a box.
- Use imagery. Imagine your Inner Critic shrinking and

place it in a matchbox. Put your Inner Critic in a boat and send it down a river. Sit your Inner Critic on a white, fluffy cloud and let it drift by.

- Turn the words of the Inner Critic into gibberish or sing them in a funny voice.
- Apologise to yourself every time you hear your Inner Critic.
- Shift your attention away from your thoughts. Notice instead what is happening around you. Focus your attention on what can you see, hear, smell, touch. This is called mindfulness, which I will explore more fully later.

THE INNER SOFTIE

There is also another part of some people's personality that is potent and impacts on their creativity. I will call this part the Inner Softie. The Inner Softie lets us off the hook whenever the going gets tough and we are challenged in some way. Heidi, a talented singer and songwriter, has an Inner Softie that seems to rule her life, particularly when it comes to getting ahead and finding work in the entertainment industry. Sometimes when Heidi thinks about composing or singing practice her Inner Softie says, 'You're too tired today, go and have a rest' or 'You only get frustrated trying to reach those high notes — you'd better leave it.' The Inner Softie sounds like it's quite supportive, but really it's not encouraging. The underlying message of the Inner Softie is that you are not capable enough or good enough to be successful. If you have a prominent Inner Softie you might have had some well-meaning but over-protective parenting. Perhaps you had a parent or parents who did everything for you. Or maybe you didn't learn how to tolerate discomfort or frustration, which are normal feelings when we learn something new.

UNMASKING YOUR INNER SOFTIE

Are you aware of an Inner Softie? Give yourself some time to do a similar exercise to the one you did for the Inner Critic. Draw your Inner Softie and write down some of the things it says to let you off the hook from pursuing your creative goals. Take yourself through some of the deflating strategies you used for the Inner Critic. They work equally well for the Inner Softie.

Okay, so what do you do now that you've identified these aspects of your personality? Besides the strategies we have already looked at, you can actively encourage two other parts of your personality that counteract the Inner Critic and Inner Softie.

What's a good name for something that is opposite to the Inner Critic? I like the name 'Inner Supporter'. And what about the opposite of the Inner Softie? How about 'Inner Guide'? You can make up your own names if you wish.

We'll explore these two new players by hearing about Mary, a high school student.

MARY

Mary is getting ready to play the piano in a school concert. Here's one way she could think beforehand: 'I stuffed it up last year, so probably will again. I'm so hopeless.' What part of her personality is operating here? Sounds like the Inner Critic, doesn't it?

What about this? 'What does it matter anyhow? I'll just get it over and done with. I've had a cold recently so I can't do my best.' Does this sound a bit soft to you?

It does to me. Her Inner Softie lets her off the hook from giving the piano recital her best shot.

Let's try out two other ways. 'Mmmmm, I know I'm nervous, but that's okay. I know I can play well.' This is her Inner Supporter. Hear how Mary is acknowledging her feelings — it's normal to feel some anxiety in this situation. Also hear how she is saying something reassuring, to trust and have faith in herself to do the best she can. This is something a supportive friend would say. Of course it's great to hear words of encouragement from friends or family, but you can give yourself this sort of support and encouragement too.

Here is another way Mary could think: 'I'll get a good night's sleep and practise again in the morning.' Again this is supportive, but it's more than that — it's also clear, logical thinking. Her Inner Guide is at work. Mary is being firm with herself and exercising self-discipline. So nurturing self-talk as well as self-discipline is vital to encouraging our own creativity.

SELF-SUPPORT

Think of a challenging creative task you want to do. Write down what your Inner Critic might say. Can you identify an Inner Softie? If so, what does this part of you say? Okay, so now imagine that you are a very supportive and caring friend.

- *What can you say to yourself that is encouraging?*
- *What can you say to be firm with yourself in this situation?*
- *What are the things you could do to help yourself*

in this situation? Be practical and constructive at
this point. This could be challenging, but it may be
the most important step on your creative journey.
Further chapters will help you to develop skills in
being both supportive and constructive.

SHOTS OF POSITIVITY

So far we have discovered several ways of dealing with unhelpful or critical self-talk. Here's a recap:

- Identifying and evaluating self-talk (Chapter Five).
- Changing self-talk into being helpful and realistic (Chapter Five).
- Identifying key players in your self-talk — the Inner Critic and the Inner Softie — and developing more encouraging players, the Inner Supporter and the Inner Guide.
- Various methods using your imagination to let go of unhelpful and critical self-talk.

Let's now look at another way to deal with negativity. This is quick and sharp and particularly helpful to give you a shot of positivity when the chips are down. This way doesn't replace what we have covered so far, but it is another powerful tool to have in your creative kit bag. I am talking about affirmations.

Affirmations

An affirmation is a powerful and empowering self-statement. It's a positive statement that something is already happening and present in yourself and/or your life; for example, 'I am creative' or 'I can do this.' An affirmation is a potent antidote to unhelpful self-talk. Sometimes people disregard using affirmations because they say they don't believe them. This is a common reaction. Your conscious mind might not believe the affirmation for some time; however, an affirmation will register in your subconscious mind. When you nourish your subconscious mind with helpful and encouraging messages and affirmations, subtle changes in yourself will occur that impact on how you feel and behave. In time your conscious mind will be more inclined to believe what you tell it. Here are some important things to remember about affirmations:

- Phrase affirmations in the present tense. Not 'I *will* be creative' but 'I *am* creative.'
- Phrase affirmations in the most positive way that you can. Affirm what you want, not what you don't want. Not 'I won't be self-critical', but 'I support and encourage my creativity.'
- In general, the shorter and simpler the affirmation, the more effective it is.
- Choose affirmations that feel right for you although, as I mentioned, it is natural to feel some resistance to begin with.

You can use affirmations in different ways:

- Repeat your affirmation or affirmations several times a day.
- Repeat them when you wake up in the morning and say them to yourself before you go to sleep at night.
- Write an affirmation on a card and place the card somewhere where you will see it frequently. Make several cards with different affirmations. You can use post-it notes and stick them up around the house!
- Write affirmations on your computer. Have them as a screen saver.

- Affirmations can be repeated out loud or thought silently to yourself.
- One very powerful way to use affirmations is to say them while looking in the mirror.
- Say them with conviction. The affirmation is even more powerful when you picture yourself in the way the affirmation suggests.

Here are some examples of affirmations:
- I allow myself to explore, play and create.
- I give myself permission to be creative.
- I nurture my creativity by ...
- I love to create.
- I am in touch with my creative energy.
- I deserve a rewarding, creative life.
- I have a constant flow of inspiring ideas.
- I am finding new ways.
- I take in interesting ideas that stimulate me.
- I've got what it takes.

Affirmations can also be short encouraging statements like, 'Let's do it', 'Keep going', 'Get into it' or 'Do it now.' These short, sharp boosts can move you forward if you are feeling reluctant or lack faith in yourself.

If you encounter a lot of internal resistance to your affirmations and your Inner Critic interferes in your attempts to be positive, take this next step. Write down the affirmation on one side of a page in your journal and on the other side list all the negative responses from your Inner Critic. Get them out of your system. See what the Inner Critic is all about and evaluate how unhelpful and untrue the Inner Critic is. Remember the skills you learnt in the last chapter and this chapter.

CREATIVE TOUCHSTONES

This chapter introduced you to different parts of your personality that have the capacity to powerfully influence how you approach and engage in your creative time. While the Inner Critic and the Inner Softie deflate your creative energy, you have found powerful tools to disarm their potency and to engage the Inner Supporter and the Inner Guide as firm dynamic allies.

This chapter also described how to use affirmations as a way to boost your creative esteem. They are just one of the many effective tools you can use on your creative journey. There will be more as we go on.

Chapter Seven

STRESS LESS, CREATE MORE

Stress is like spice — in the right proportion
it enhances the flavour of the dish.
Too little produces a bland, dull meal,
too much may choke you.

— DONALD TUBESING

Stress is often proclaimed as the modern epidemic of our society. Most of us have experienced either a short-term taste of stress overload or perhaps a longer bout that has impacted more severely on our health and wellbeing. This chapter helps you to understand your stress triggers and your usual response to stressful situations. Through this insight you will be guided in developing your own stress management strategies. This is important because too much stress will squash your creative expression. We will also look at two underlying causes for stress: discouragement and criticism from others. And finally, in this chapter you'll learn a short calming technique called centring that you can use at any time and any place to lower your experience of stress.

WHAT IS STRESS?

We need to manage our stress, not just for our health, but because it can erode every part of our life, including our creative expression. We can't expect ourselves to function creatively under enormous sustained pressure. And that's what stress is: pressure. Too much pressure stops the flow of our creativity energy.

At its simplest, stress is what happens in our bodies and in our minds when there is some sort of challenge or demand. It's a normal reaction when we are under pressure, such as rushing to meet a deadline or running to catch a bus. Once the deadline is met or you are sitting on the bus, hopefully the stress reaction settles. The same reaction happens when we perform (act, play, sing) or attend the opening of our first art exhibition or book launch (let's be positive!). It's a natural and necessary function of the body to deal with a situation that is more demanding than usual.

Of course, there are times in our lives when there is more serious stress than running to catch a bus or performing on stage. Perhaps we lose a job, move house or we experience the ending of a relationship — these are life events that need time and energy to adjust to. And sometimes there are too many stressors to handle and we experience stress overload. Remember though that response to stress is individual. What one person finds stressful another person may not.

What happens in our body when we are stressed?

When we are stressed our body works harder in all sorts of ways. There is an increase in heart rate and blood pressure and our muscles tense. Our breathing becomes faster and there is an increase in stress hormones and chemicals within our blood stream. It's often called the fight or flight response because it's a life-saving, in-built mechanism that we have had since early times to deal with threat. The stress reaction prepares us to run away or fight for survival. Some stress is also necessary to motivate us to do things that are important to us, such as our creative work. Stress stimulates adrenaline, noradrenaline and glucose to flow into our blood, which in turn gives us the buzz or energy to be creative. If there were no stress at all we would be so laid back that nothing would get done. So a manageable amount of stress is fine. The key, though, is for the stress reaction not to be too high and for it to settle once the situation is over.

The stress reaction can also occur due to perceived demands, such as thinking about showing your poetry to a friend. Imagining something scary is enough to trigger the fight or flight response. The mind can start saying things such as, 'It won't be good enough' or 'She'll think it's awful.' We can wind up the stress reaction in our body through our self-talk. We often call this type of stress anxiety.

Too much stress

Let's read about Declan, who has a number of stressors in his life.

DECLAN

Declan wants to sculpt. He does the occasional weekend workshop and wants to spend more time in his shed experimenting with some ideas for making a sculpture for his garden. He works full time and does an enormous amount of community work. He often races from one meeting to the next, takes work home and does very little exercise. He believes that being busy is exercise enough. He notices he often feels tense, especially in his shoulders and jaw. He sleeps badly. He wakes up worrying about all the things he needs to get done. He feels tired a lot of the time and he is often irritable, especially towards his partner. Declan is suffering from stress overload. There are a number of stressors impacting on him and they are leading to anxious thoughts: 'I'm losing it' and 'I can't handle things like I used to.' Once upon a time he considered himself a really together person, but now he is worried that things are falling apart. He can't concentrate as he used to and his thoughts are becoming increasingly negative. He has also lost his drive to go into his shed to sculpt.

As you can see there are too many demands on Declan. Stress is impacting on him in four main areas:

- *Physically:* He is tired and suffers from muscle tension. He sleeps badly.
- *Mentally:* He worries excessively. His mind is constantly busy with what he has to do. His self-talk is unhelpful and he finds it hard to concentrate.
- *Emotionally:* He is irritable and short tempered.
- *Behaviourally:* He 'races' from one thing to the next. He doesn't exercise or give himself time to relax. He doesn't go to his shed anymore to sculpt.

Declan needs to make some changes. If he doesn't, he may suffer more serious consequences, such as ill health and relationship problems.

What about you?

Are you aware of feeling stressed? Do you identify in any way with Declan? I hope not, but if you do there are many ways you can help yourself to lower your current level of stress. First, try the following quiz.

STRESS QUIZ

Read through the following eight statements and answer with a 'Yes', 'No' or 'Sometimes'.

1. *Do you find that your mind is constantly busy thinking about all the things that must be done?*
2. *Do you find that you are prone to worrying and feeling anxious?*
3. *Are you drinking more alcohol to help you relax; eating for comfort or using some other form of 'relaxant', such as cigarettes, marijuana or another drug?*
4. *Do you find that you are feeling less sociable than usual, not wanting to be bothered with family and friends?*
5. *Do you have difficulty falling asleep or wake up in the night and find your mind is busy with worries and things to do? Or conversely are you sleeping more than usual?*
6. *Do you find that you are more irritable than usual, perhaps snappy with people around you?*
7. *Do you experience muscle tension, especially in your neck, back and jaw? Do you experience tension headaches?*
8. *Do you suffer from symptoms of Irritable Bowel*

Syndrome (IBS), such as constipation and/or diarrhoea that become exacerbated when you feel stressed?

Saying 'Yes' or 'Sometimes' to any of these statements is a warning sign that stress might be impacting on your life. The more times you answered positively, the higher the degree of stress is likely to be in your life and the more likely it is to be impacting on your creative expression. The above symptoms might also indicate some sort of medical condition, so it's always advisable to get checked out by a doctor. If you said 'No' to all of the above, it sounds like you have a well-balanced life and that you are managing the ups and downs that come your way. You are likely to be enjoying your creative interests.

Stress management

We all need to build into our lives some general stress management strategies. There is nothing particularly complex about them; they are about making sure you have a healthy balance in your life and include our natural needs for living well:

- healthy food
- adequate sleep
- relaxation
- exercise
- family time
- friendships
- time for nature and/or spirituality
- and time for whatever else that's important to you and fits with the values you highlighted in Chapter One.

In previous chapters we looked at how our thinking patterns

increase stress and anxiety. You found ways to be aware of your self-talk and then challenged and changed it so it became helpful and supportive. So now we will look at some practical and physical ways to handle stress.

Exercise is an excellent antidote to stress. It helps us to manage the level of cortisol in our body, a chemical that is elevated in people who are chronically stressed. Exercise also increases endorphin release, which is the body's own pain-relieving and mood-elevating chemical. And it releases muscle tension that has built up in the body. For some people, jogging or other aerobic exercise provides the stress release they need. Others find yoga or Tai Chi more appealing. Or you can enjoy a mixture of exercise options that includes sports such as tennis or squash. It's worth persevering until you find what works well for you and fits in with your lifestyle.

Having a massage or a relaxing bath can help to release tension, while watching funny films and having a laugh releases pent-up stress too. Understandably, it's important to get an adequate amount of sleep at night, to eat well and to maintain a healthy weight.

Mentally, meditation or relaxation exercises help you to let go of tension (the last chapter of the book expands on this idea). Emotionally you need to tune in to your body and listen to how you feel. If you feel down or anxious, journal and/or talk to someone you trust. If you feel sad, have a good cry. Channel your feelings into your creative domain. Write about your feelings in a poem or song or express how you feel in a painting. Dance to your emotions. Find a way to honour where you are at and give your feelings some expression or else they will feed your stress level.

What else can help? Give some thought to your individual traits. Find out what your creative rhythms are. When do you seem to work and play best? Are you a morning person or an evening person? Do you like to create indoors or outdoors? Do you need to take yourself away for some time of solitude to create? Or conversely do you need to meet up with some like-minded people to 'play' together?

SELF-CARE STRATEGIES

Stress management strategies fall under the umbrella of self-care. Self-care is important in preventing stress overload, as well as being absolutely essential if stress has started to get a grip on your life and is impacting on your creative expression. Let's now work out your personal strategy for self-care. Whether you are going well or feel a little or a lot stressed, this will help you to discover your own self-care tool kit.

The creative well

I like to use the metaphor of our body and mind being like a deep well. It's perhaps a bit odd, but I find that thinking symbolically often helps you to see yourself in a new way. Imagine that when you are full of clear, refreshing water you cope well with the everyday demands of life. You feel inspired and have much to draw on to nourish your creative expression. When your well is three-quarters full you feel less motivated, have less energy and perhaps are even a bit down on yourself. When your well is half full and being depleted, you feel even more discouraged, perhaps avoiding creative expression and feeling some of the symptoms of stress. If your well is only a quarter full, you are in dangerous territory: you are likely to be experiencing stress overload or possibly be engaging in self-sabotaging behaviour that interferes with your creativity, such as abusing drugs or staying in a destructive relationship. You are not likely to be living according to what you really value in life. Your self-care strategies at this level are very low.

Let's have a look at Dario's creative well as he sets out to do some outdoor sketching.

DARIO

Dario wakes up keen to get into his art one Saturday morning, but feels his energy flagging as he packs up his gear. He wonders what could be getting in the way. He's annoyed because finally he has a morning to himself as his children are with his ex-wife. He can't understand his change of heart. He hasn't been particularly stressed, but has noticed a few changes. He is bringing more work home, not sleeping as well and generally he is a bit more irritable.

Dario needs to ask himself four important questions. They might seem like common sense, but when we are down or stressed we often sidestep the obvious and move into unhelpful mind chatter that exacerbates how we feel.

Dario's questions and answers

1. Where is my creative energy right now, on a scale of 1 to 10 with 1 being low and 10 being the highest? 5 — Dario's well is only half full.

2. What brings my creative energy down? Not getting enough sleep, too much work, not exercising, listening to my Inner Critic, fighting with the kids.

3. What can I do to raise the level of my creative energy? Get more sleep, start going for walks again, give myself encouraging self-talk, think of some pleasant things to do with the kids. Not sure what to do about the work situation.

4. What will I do TODAY to make a start? I'll walk to the park, rather than drive. I can use my backpack to take my drawing material. When the kids come tomorrow, we'll decide on something enjoyable to do together.

Dario is problem solving by deliberately addressing his stress triggers and making decisions that are aligned with his values. Remember that values are those ways of being or living that are meaningful to us. For Dario his top values are his relationship with his children, his health and his creativity. Dario doesn't have to fix everything at once, but he starts with what's most important. By starting there, it's likely to help with some of the other issues too. Exercise will help his sleep and mood. Having some fun with his children will also help with his mood. By writing things down, he starts to see clearly what's bothering him. He's not sure what to do about the work he brings home, but at least he has been honest with himself by recognising it's become a problem he will need to address.

What about you?

You can't expect the best of yourself creatively if you are not looking after your health and other important areas of your life. It's like assuming your car will run well when you don't do the required maintenance and pump up the tyres. It just won't perform in these circumstances. It often takes just one change to make a difference to how you feel and this is then likely to stimulate you to make another change. One step at a time! In the following exercise I ask you to imagine you are like a deep well. Allow yourself to have this creative image, but if this symbol doesn't work for you, that's okay, you can still answer the questions.

YOUR CREATIVE WELL

In your journal draw your own well. If you are unsure how to draw a well, a cylinder or even a rectangle will be fine.

Where is your creative energy level right now? *Draw a line on your well to indicate your level. Remember that 1 is the lowest and 10 is at the top of your well. If it is over 8.5, well done! What are you doing to take care of yourself to keep your creative energy at such a terrific level? What are your self-care strategies? Write about them in your journal. It's great to acknowledge what's working well. It will be helpful to read your list if things start to change.*

If your creative energy level is lower than 8.5 ask yourself: **What brings my creative energy down?** *Sometimes it helps to look at different areas of your life. Home life? Work life? Social life? Creative life? Physical health, such as exercise and time for relaxation? Spiritual life? Relationships? Mental or emotional health, such as possible depression, anxiety or awareness of a tyrannical Inner Critic? Think about each area in your life and how you feel each area is going.* **What can you do to raise the level of your creative well?** *What do you see as your priority at this time? Do you need to revisit the Values exercise you did in Chapter One* *to remind you of what's really important? Jot down some things you can do that can help in one or two areas of your life.*

What will you do today to make a start? *It helps to make a contract with yourself regarding what you will do. I suggest you write this in your journal. When you write a contract write it in positive language. You can start with: 'I have made a decision to do the following to take care of my creative energy ...'*

It's helpful to do this exercise again in a week's time and see whether there's been an increase in your creative energy. If not, you may find the exercises in the following chapter will help you further, particularly the exercises on setting goals and another in-depth problem solving exercise.

DEALING WITH OTHER PEOPLE'S DISCOURAGEMENT

Another source of stress for many creative people is dealing with others who are discouraging and critical. Let's look at discouragement first. Discouragers say things like, 'You won't be able to do that' or 'That's a silly idea' or 'You're wasting your time.' Discouragers are sometimes just very negative people, perhaps jealous you are pursuing opportunities and taking risks they secretly wish they had the courage to do. However, sometimes discouragers believe that what they are saying is for your own good. They could be fearful you might not be successful and could get hurt and disappointed. In their offbeat way they are trying to protect you. So be careful who you talk to about your creativity and your projects. Only tell people you think will be supportive and encouraging. Or if you think your family member or friend is trying to be well meaning, explain to them why your creativity is so important to you and ask them for what you need instead; for example, some encouragement.

DEALING WITH OTHER PEOPLE'S CRITICISM

Do you feel deflated when people criticise your work? Perhaps even shattered? Once you embark on your creative journey, there is a good chance you will receive some criticism in one form or another. This is a necessary part of fine-tuning your skills. Whether you join a class, a choir, a writers' group or receive feedback from your family or friends, you can find ways to hear the criticism so that it's helpful rather than leaving you feeling torn to shreds.

Of course, there is a big difference between constructive, helpful criticism and destructive criticism. Constructive criticism is given in the spirit of helping you improve your skills or performance. It's given in a way that is not directed at your worth as a person, but rather at the creative task and how it might be improved. Let's look at some examples of criticism. Read through the following statements and decide whether you think they are constructive or destructive.

1. 'Great song, although I think the other one suits the timbre of your voice.'
2. 'This poem is really powerful. I wonder about the ending and whether you might consider ...'
3. 'What about using a cooler glaze inside the bowl?'
4. 'That painting looks really strange.'
5. 'I can't see the point in taking photos of nuts and bolts.'
6. 'You're just an amateur, aren't you? But at least you're trying.'

7. 'What's the point of starting to write now? You're too old.'

What did you decide? The first three statements are constructive because they invite the person to consider something that might improve their work. As the creator, you can use this feedback or not. Statements 4 and 5 are rather negative and the last two statements are definitely destructive. You need to protect yourself from negative and destructive criticism, to see it for what it is and not dwell on it. That's sometimes easier said than done, I know, particularly if the criticism comes from people you live with or are close to.

It's not within the scope of this book to give assertiveness a lot of time, and there are many assertiveness techniques that you can find in books or on the Internet. However, I'd like to share one of my favourite techniques, called an 'I' message. When you give an 'I' message, you tell the person how you feel about their particular behaviour in a clear and respectful way. You can also let them know what you would like instead. Let's have a look at the last statement: 'What's the point of starting to write now? You're too old.'

Now you could get angry and be unkind too, or you can take a deep breath and say something like: 'When you comment about my age, *I feel* discouraged/hurt/irritated [whatever you are feeling], and *what I would like* is some support instead.'

You may not get what you ask for, but at least you let the person know how you feel. You can then choose whether you share your creativity with them in future.

Criticism that pushes a button

Sometimes when we receive constructive criticism we hear it as being negative and feel hurt and even defensive. When this happens the criticism usually 'pushes' an internal emotional button, an unconscious vulnerability that we are not even aware of. Let me tell you about Clem.

CLEM

Clem has started drawing classes. She enjoyed drawing when she was younger, but stopped when she was a teenager because of a particularly negative and critical art teacher. She forgot about the pleasure drawing gave her until she saw an ad in the newspaper for art classes. She decided to give it another try. In the first class they did a still-life drawing. Her teacher gave her praise and encouragement and also made a suggestion about shading and tone. This feedback hit the 'sore spot' that had been buried for many years. Clem, like a lot of people, didn't take on board the positives from her teacher, but dwelled on what she saw as the negative; that is, she didn't know about shading and tone. She filtered out the positives and made the assumption that she couldn't draw at all.

When we are learning new skills we need feedback and constructive criticism. If it hits an emotional 'sore spot', give yourself some time to think about where this might come from. Journalling is a helpful tool. Just writing or drawing about your recent experience and feelings may trigger where in your past or who in your past might have originally hurt you. You might have become aware of some of these unhelpful messages or criticism in Chapter Three when you did the exercise 'Discovering messages from the past'. Once discovered, you are more able to address the criticism in the present, especially when you engage your Inner Supporter and your ability to be self-compassionate. Besides journalling, it's often helpful to talk to a friend or perhaps a counsellor to help you clear up some of these historical 'hurts' that are still impacting on you today.

Another helpful strategy is to write a 'letter' to the person in the past who hurt you and tell them how you feel and what you are doing to move forward. The letter can be written in your journal or on paper that you can keep, burn or tear up. This is often a significant ritual that can feel cathartic and liberating. The letter is not intended to be sent to the person, but for you to get things off your chest and to honour what you are doing now on your creative journey. It's very empowering. Here is what Clem wrote to her high school art teacher:

Dear Mr Bates

I remember how you used to pick away at my drawings, saying they weren't right and that I wasn't looking properly at what I was drawing. I didn't like the way you stood over me, making me feel small time and time again. Well, you know Mr Bates, I can still hear your picky voice, but I'm not going to take any more notice. I really like going to my drawing class and I'm going to enjoy it and keep learning and appreciate my own style and allow it to develop.

COURAGEOUS CREATIVITY

It's comfortable staying with what we know rather than delving into the unknown. It helps to keep us feeling competent and sure about who we are and what we do. In contrast, exploring something new can make us feel uncertain and anxious at times. We can have doubts: 'Can I do this?' or 'What will others think?' It takes courage to hang in there, experience our feelings and give ourselves the opportunity to reap the rewards and joy that come from creating. Sometimes there are also expectations from others that we will produce something 'special' straightaway. It takes courage to show friends and family the landscape you have been painting at art class, your first woodwork creation or a short story you have been writing. While most people are encouraging and supportive, some can respond with surprise or even disappointment. You can almost hear them thinking, 'That's amateurish — I thought he said he was an artist!' or 'She reckons she can write?' They seem to think you should be at a 'high' standard from the start. So again, be careful with whom you share. Remember that it takes time to build up your skills and creative flair.

Can you think of times when you were courageous? Perhaps starting a new job, course of study or joining a group? You probably remember feeling some anxiety mixed in with excitement. We can feel the same when starting a new creative path as well as many times along the way in our creative expression. So remember your past courage as you continue to create.

CENTRING

This chapter concludes with a helpful short relaxation exercise that can be used anywhere and at any time as a means of lowering the level of stress in your body. This exercise is particularly helpful if you are feeling agitated and can't seem to settle into your creative time. When we feel stressed, we often say things like, 'I feel all over the place' or 'I just can't get my head together' or 'My heart feels like it's jumping out of my chest.' When we feel anxious we breathe faster and in a shallow way rather than using all of our lungs. We also tense our body, particularly our jaw and shoulder muscles. We have turned on the fight or flight reaction I talked about earlier. Centring is a way to change what is happening in our bodies in a few easy steps.

Step One:	Stop what you are doing. Sit down if you can. Keep your back straight, relax your shoulders without slumping forward and relax your jaw muscles. Feel the support of the floor under your feet. Rest your hands in your lap.
Step Two:	Start by taking two slow, slightly deeper breaths. Breaths that allow your abdomen to expand. This means you are filling all of your lungs, not just the top half. You might want to place a hand gently on your abdomen, so you can check that you are breathing from this place.
Step Three:	Continue to breathe comfortably into your abdomen and notice the slight rise and fall. This is your centre. This is what grounds you and settles you.
Step Four:	After a few breaths, say, 'R-e-l-a-x' slowly on the breath out. Let the breath out be slightly longer than the breath in. Notice the natural pause after the breath in and the breath out.
Step Five:	As you continue to breathe, pay particular attention to your jaw and shoulders. If you notice any area of tension in your body, imagine that you can breathe gently in and out of this part.
Step Six:	It's normal to become distracted by thoughts and other things. Just notice when this happens and come back and focus on your breathing.

Practise centring as often as you can because you will then find it easier to use at times when you are feeling stressed. Aim to do it at least once a day so you get to know what it feels like. You can do it for two minutes or ten minutes. It's up to you, but regular practice will give you a lifelong strategy to help with stress.

CREATIVE TOUCHSTONES

We often expect too much of ourselves, but if we are tired, unfit or stressed it's like running up a hill without breakfast or proper running shoes. You might get there eventually, but not without greater difficulty and perhaps even damage. Self-care is essential to keep you healthy so you can engage in your creative interests. So keep your creative well as full as possible. This helps in all sorts of ways, including dealing with other people's discouragement and criticism. In this chapter you have also learnt how to relax your body and mind through centring, which is an excellent antidote to stress.

Let's now move on to your creative goals.

Chapter Eight

STEPPING YOURSELF TO SUCCESS

No great thing is created suddenly.

— EPICTETUS

Seeing yourself successfully achieve what you desire is exciting, isn't it? Perhaps you're picturing:

- writing five poems that express your love of nature
- learning how to tango
- joining a dramatic society and acting on stage.

Or maybe your picture is bigger:

- painting stunning landscapes for an art exhibition
- taking distinctive and beautiful photos for an art competition
- singing and receiving appreciative applause
- writing a book people want to read.

It's great to dream your 'big picture' but at the same time sometimes we can feel overwhelmed: 'How on earth am I going to get there?' We might feel like giving up without even taking the first steps. This chapter looks at how we move along our creative journey, step by step. You will have the opportunity to look at your long-term goals and then break them down into medium- and short-term goals. This makes your journey do-able. Step by step you get to where you want to go.

WHY GOALS?

For some people, having goals seems to be the antithesis of what creativity is all about. They say, 'Isn't it about freedom and spontaneity?' But having goals doesn't mean that spontaneity is thwarted or that freedom is absent. Goals, no matter how small or large, provide an impetus and motivation to move forward. They can range from being specific, such as, 'This afternoon I will rehearse my song for the performance tonight' to something that is freer: 'This afternoon I will improvise and play with different keys and see what emerges.' Here, there is spontaneity within the structure of setting a goal.

DIFFERENT TYPES OF GOALS

Our goals can be divided into three categories: long, medium and short term. We'll take a look at each in turn.

Long-term goals

A long-term goal is our broad vision for the future. We are more likely to be successful when we have a clear sense or a picture of what we want to achieve over a period of time. However, this picture should not be too specific or rigid. It's reasonable to be open to other possibilities along the way. In the next exercise I ask you to fantasise about your long-term goals by writing a letter to yourself from the future. This exercise is often used in coaching psychology and helps to clarify your hopes, dreams and what you truly desire for yourself. First, read through the following two examples to get an idea of what I mean.

JAMES

The following letter is from James, who at fifty-five years of age owns a successful business and writes fiction from time to time. He wants to pursue his writing more vigilantly. In his letter he is imagining that he is writing it on his sixtieth birthday and reviewing the previous five years.

Dear James

Here I am on my sixtieth birthday and I'm glad to say my life has really turned around in the last five years. Five years ago I was working a 60-hour week, squeezing in time with my wife and kids and trying to write occasionally. I've changed all that. I now work only 35–40 hours each week. I've put aside regular hours to sit down to write and I've gone to several writing workshops. I've learnt a lot. I really believe in myself now and I have stopped putting myself down and thinking my writing is rubbish. I have submitted my short stories to various competitions and I've had one accepted for publication. I'm looking forward to what the next five years will bring!

Here is another example from Clare.

CLARE

Clare has always wanted to learn how to make ceramic pots. She remembers enjoying the feelings associated with manipulating clay in art class when she was at school and the pleasure of making simple pots. Clare is seventy-two years old and recently lost her husband to cancer. In her letter from the future, she is imagining that she is eighty and looking back over the previous eight years.

Dear Clare

Good on you! At first you thought you were too old to start something new, didn't you? You found it hard to get out of the house after Ted died, but you took a chance and went along to that first pottery class with Isabel. Remember those early pots and how exciting it was to see them come out of the kiln? You have stuck with it over the years and have made so many beautiful gifts. You enjoy giving away the things you make to others. You have even been part of the local art exhibition. You miss Ted, but you have discovered something that you never dreamed possible when he was alive.

LETTER FROM THE FUTURE

Now it's your turn to write a letter! Give yourself the freedom to be positive and encouraging. Be wary of that Inner Critic who might step in and give you a hard time. Just let that Inner Critic go and focus on this fantasy exercise. Choose a time in the future, perhaps a significant birthday, and write a letter to yourself from that date, looking back over the previous years. Write about what you have achieved. Go on, give it a try and enjoy!

Long-term goals inspire us to move forward. We develop a purpose for our creativity. However, we need to be open to the possibility that we might decide to change course or even the destination. This is not a sign of failure. As we progress towards a goal we naturally have many experiences and meet different people — all of which can have an influence on our own creative path. It's possible we might change our mind and decide to follow a different path. For example, Josh had been a successful songwriter for a couple of bands. He also liked to sing, but he hadn't considered himself a singer. However, one night he was asked to step in for a band member who was sick. It was his first experience of singing his songs to an audience and he found he loved it! This was an important experience that triggered changing his career direction to include singing.

MEDIUM-TERM GOALS

The timeframe for medium-term goals will vary from person to person. These goals focus on what we want to achieve in a shorter period of time, such as a week, a month, six months or even a year. Similar to the exercise you have just done, it's helpful to project yourself into the future and think about what it is you want to achieve. When you set goals it's important to make sure they are realistic and achievable. If you set yourself an impossible task you will end up feeling discouraged, so you need to set SMART goals. SMART stands for **S**pecific, **M**easurable, **A**ttractive, **R**ealistic and **T**imeframed. Let's have a look at each part in turn.

Specific

Specific goals give us a clear sense of direction for what we want to achieve. Here are some examples. Mykos says, 'By the end of the year I want to have a rough draft of my book written.' Jan decides, 'I will practise playing the guitar five days a week for half an hour.' Gabrielle says, 'I will give myself two hours each weekend to experiment with different painting mediums.' Each of these three goals makes it clear what the person wants to accomplish.

Measurable

How will you know whether you have achieved your goal? We need to be able to measure or evaluate what we have done. In the above examples, it will be clear whether the goals have been accomplished. Mykos will actually see his draft in front of him at the end of the year. Jan decides she will put ticks on her calendar after each practice and thus will easily see if she has achieved her goal at the end of each week. She will also be able to reflect on the skills she has learnt over that period of time. Gabrielle will see the fruits of creative play each weekend to show she has been experimenting with her art materials.

Attractive

We need to make sure the goal is something we really want to do. It helps to be aware of all the benefits in achieving your goal. If you are in doubt, I suggest you write in your journal all the positives you will experience from accomplishing your goal. Mykos says, 'In seeing the draft in front of me I will feel that I'm at last taking myself seriously. I will feel really good that I have stuck with it and I'll be ready to work on polishing the draft in the following year.' Jan writes in her journal, 'By regularly playing the guitar for half an hour a day, I'll love being able to play more tunes.' Gabrielle says, 'This goal of experimenting with my art materials will help me feel more confident and I'll enjoy seeing what I've created.' Mykos, Jan and Gabrielle are making sure their goals are attractive.

Realistic

We also need to make sure the goal is achievable. If we don't have the time and the resources, we are setting ourselves up for failure, which is naturally de-motivating. In order to make his goal realistic, Mykos cuts down on his television watching and thus frees up time at night and on weekends to write. Jan decides to give herself a half hour of practice by getting up early and, if this doesn't happen, to forgo watching the news at night. Gabrielle feels confident that she can find two hours on the weekend for her experimentation. All three have thought through their goals and feel that they are do-able.

Timeframed

Timeframes help with motivation and keep us on target. We ask ourselves, 'When do I want to achieve this goal?' Mykos already has a timeframe for the end of the year. Jan and Gabrielle need to build into their goal-setting a date in the future to review their goals and see if they have achieved what they set out to do. Jan, the guitar player, decides to review her goal after four weeks. This is what she wrote in her journal: 'This feels great. I've managed to practise five times a week. My repertoire has increased from four songs to ten.' Gabrielle decides to review her goal after two months. She reflects in her journal that she enjoyed her two hours every weekend so much that she often spends much longer. By having a review date Jan and Gabrielle see that they are both achieving what they set out to do. Of course, if this were not the case, the next step would be to make some changes to ensure the goals were SMART.

YOUR SMART GOALS

It's now your turn to set yourself some SMART medium-term goals. In your journal write down two or three medium-term goals. First, think about your long-term vision and then think of goals that will move you in this direction. They might be just ideas floating around in your head or particular goals you feel sure about. If you need to, give yourself a few days to allow them to form. And then, when you are ready, pick one of these medium-term goals and make it SMART:

S – *Specific: What is it in particular you want to achieve?*

M – *Measurable: How will you know you've reached your goal? Do you need to include how often? How much?*

A – *Attractive: Is this goal something you really want to give time to? What do you like about this goal?*

R – *Realistic: Is your goal sensible? Is it something that you think with effort you will be able to achieve? Do you have the time? How will you make the time?*

T – *Timeframed: What length of time will you give yourself to achieve this goal? Make a date in the future to review what you achieve over this period. Perhaps write this review date on your calendar or in your diary.*

Short-term goals

Short-term goals are about what you want to accomplish in a creative session. This session may be as short as an hour or longer, say a day or a weekend. When you are working on a specific project, hopefully you have ideas about where you want to go next. Let's follow Mykos, Jan and Gabrielle and see how they managed their short-term goals.

Mykos, the writer, sets himself different goals depending on where he is up to in his writing. At times he sets himself a goal to write about 300 words in an evening. At other times, he sets himself a goal to do some research. He is writing a murder mystery and there are certain things he needs to check out, such as how to go about falsifying a passport. At other times he sets himself a goal of re-reading a chapter to make some changes. Each time he sits down to write he has a clear idea of what he wants to achieve.

Jan, the guitar player, first practises the easier chords and then plays certain chords together. Sometimes she sets herself a goal of experimenting in different ways to phrase the music. Finally she progresses to playing the whole song.

Gabrielle also sets herself a goal each weekend. Sometimes she experiments with different mediums or copies an artist she admires. At other times she sets up a still-life to paint or goes to a favourite spot in the country to sketch. She has direction to help her make a start on her project, and because her whole aim is to be experimental, she also feels at liberty to change course.

WHAT IF I GET STUCK ON MY GOALS?

Feeling stuck or having a period of inactivity is a normal part of the creative process. It's important to be kind to yourself and accept what is happening rather than beat up on yourself. It happens to us all. Here is a problem-solving exercise that poses several questions to help you sort out if there is something in particular that is leading you to feel stuck. This process is an extension of the creative well exercise from the previous chapter. It provides you with the opportunity to think of options and plan some helpful strategies to move forward. First of all, let's look at some questions that can help as a creative problem-solving process and then we will look at an example.

The questions

- What's happening to me right now in my creative process?
- How long has it been a problem?
- How am I feeling about it?
- How important on a scale of 1 to 10 is it to resolve this?
- What could be impacting on me at this time and affecting my creative expression?
- Is there something in particular that I need to attend to?
- What are my options? (Always be very flexible in looking at options. Even jot down silly ones.)
- What am I willing to do about this problem? What options look best for me right now?
- What are the pros and cons of putting this option into place?
- What are my personal resources/skills to put this option into place?
- Do I need help? Who might help?
- When will I do this?

Now let's have a look at how Joe, a retired man who loves writing short stories, responded to these questions.

JOE

Joe looks after his wife, who has had a stroke. Each week he makes use of some respite care and often goes to the library. He usually enjoys writing in the afternoons while his wife sleeps, but has recently felt less motivated. He is not sure why. Going through this creative problem-solving exercise might help Joe to sort out what is going on. Here are his answers.

What's happening to me right now in my creative process? I feel stuck. Tired and flat. I miss writing and how I looked at things.

How long has it been a problem? About a month.

How am I feeling about it? It's a real shame. Sad.

How important on a scale of 1 to 10 is it to resolve this problem? I suppose it's about an 8.

What could be impacting on me at this time and affecting my creative expression? Annette's got the 'flu. I get tired. Ben and Ros next door have left.

Is there something in particular that I need to attend to? Maybe I need to find some other company. It used to be okay when Ben and Ros lived next door, but since they left … yes, that's probably when I started to feel lonely.

What are my options? (Remember, always be very flexible when looking at options. Even jot down silly ones.)

Run away!
- Maybe I should go on a holiday — a cruise maybe?
- Visit the kids in Queensland?

- Get some new friends.
- Maybe join the writers' group in town.

What am I willing to do about this problem? What options look best for me right now? Can't do the cruise — money is too tight. The writers' group is free, so they said in the pamphlet. I could just go on Tuesday and see what it's like. The respite lady has already said she can come in for two more hours each week.

What are the pros and cons of putting this option into place? Pros: I'll have some company. Meet new people. May get some ideas for the story I'm stuck on. Cons: Meeting new people ... get a bit nervous ... I can always come home, I guess.

What are my personal resources/skills to put this option into place? Well, I guess I'm pretty good at talking to people. I tend to make people laugh. Maybe I could even help others with their writing.

Do I need help? Who could help? I could ring my sister in Brazil. She always gives me a good boost. She's a happy thing.

Are there steps you need to take? When will you do these steps?

1. I'll ring my sister tonight.
2. I'll ring the Writers' Centre and check what I need to bring.
3. I'll talk to Jane tomorrow and see if she can do Tuesdays.
4. I'll talk to Annette at dinner tonight.

At Joe's first meeting at the Writers' Centre they were asked to write a short humorous anecdote. Joe's story got the biggest laugh. A couple of the younger writers asked him for coffee at a café, but he didn't stay long; he was keen to get home and jot down a few things for the 'stuck' bit of his half-written short story.

CREATING WITH OTHERS

As you can see from reading about Joe, joining others can be beneficial in boosting your creativity as you receive support and encouragement. I love my Friday art class and seeing the different ways in which we each approach the same subject, such as a landscape or a portrait. Every painting is different and reflects the gift within each of us. We support each other's uniqueness and give constructive feedback. We also learn from each other and borrow ideas and techniques that we would like to try out. So ask yourself whether you need to spend time with like-minded others. Perhaps you could join your local writers' group or find out what craft groups are available in your area? Perhaps join a choir? A theatre group? Or find someone you can meet with regularly to share creative ideas?

I know that sometimes it can be challenging joining a group, particularly if you are shy. It's often simply a matter of taking a deep breath and just going along the first time, knowing that in time it will become easier, more enjoyable and stimulating. Being with others can also trigger your Inner Critic, who likes to compare what you do with other people's accomplishments. Be aware of this typical tactic of the Inner Critic. Let it go! If you must compare, then compare yourself to no one but you! Notice the improvements and new skills development that you achieve over time.

CELEBRATING AND REWARDING OUR ACHIEVEMENTS

We all like to be rewarded, especially after we have worked hard. Rewards are intrinsic in encouraging any behaviour we want to do more of. We don't need rewards all the time because often the nature of our creative expression is, in itself, enough. But sometimes, in order to encourage ourselves to be persistent and regular in our creative expression, rewards can help. If you are working particularly hard on a project and you get to the end, find a way to celebrate. Or even after achieving a small but challenging goal find a way to acknowledge what you have achieved. Share it with a family member or a friend. Go out for a coffee or for a drink. Indulge yourself with a chocolate or a special pleasurable experience.

CREATIVE TOUCHSTONES

In developing our creativity it's important not to get overwhelmed by the big picture. We need to break down our picture into small steps. Like a jigsaw puzzle, there are many pieces that make up the whole. We can focus on one piece at a time.

Getting stuck at times is part of being human. It's normal! This chapter has shown you a straightforward problem-solving exercise to help you sort out any issues that might get in the way of achieving your goals. This is empowering and takes you closer to your vision.

In the next chapter you will find some clever ways to make use of short amounts of time and how to keep your motivation going.

Chapter Nine

CREATIVE PLAY-DATES

*Play with colour, form, light,
shadows, space, sound, words, silence, taste,
smells. Everywhere is a playground.*

— MICHAEL JOSEPH

While it is important to establish routines and helpful strategies, we also need to play. There is a delicate balance between the discipline of setting and achieving goals and the pleasure and joy that is part of the creative journey. When we are too intent on trying to get it 'right' we lose our sense of play. I love the word 'play' because as soon as I hear the word it frees me up. As you have discovered throughout this book, the words we use influence how we feel and what we ultimately do. In this chapter we'll look at some practicalities for how to make time to engage in our creativity and how to be inventive in using even small amounts of time — playfully. We will also look at two different types of motivation and how they influence our creative time.

FINDING TIME

Perhaps you feel you don't have enough time. You know you want to explore your creativity but you're not sure how you will find space in your week. The following exercise helps you to clearly see how you already spend your time. This can assist you in making decisions to find time for your regular creative play-dates. These play-dates are times for the short-term goals we looked at in the previous chapter. They take you forward in achieving your medium- and long-term goals.

HOW I USE MY TIME

Turn your journal so the length of the page is facing you. Now divide the page into eight columns. In the first column write 'Time' and then write the seven days of the week at the top of the remaining seven columns. Under 'Time' write down each hour of your waking day and you'll end up with a time grid of your week. Now take yourself through the following steps for each day in each column:

1. *Write in all your commitments — work, classes, meetings, children's activities, sport, time with family, and so on.*
2. *Next write down other activities you usually do — exercise, travel, house cleaning, sport, gardening, watching TV, meeting friends. I understand each week is different but this exercise will give you an idea of your typical week.*
3. *Now look at your lifestyle and demands with a view to giving creative time emphasis, and reflect on the following questions:*
   - *Have you got spaces in your timetable for your creativity?*

- *Is your week jam-packed with activities?*
- *Is there something that needs to change? Perhaps there is something you need to give up? Do you need to negotiate with someone to find extra time?*
- *When can you give yourself time for creative expression? The amount of time for each person is different and I don't want to be prescriptive about what you should give, but ideally, make a creative play-date at least once or twice a week. Or you might need to give yourself more time — perhaps you are a professional artist or writer or getting ready for an exhibition or a concert. It will depend on many things, including what stage you are up to in your creative journey and your commitments. But make sure you give yourself some time. Use a calendar and write in your creative goals to keep you on track.*

CREATIVE SPEED-DATES

Even really busy people have small chunks of available time in their week when they can tune into their creative expression. This next exercise asks you to find little bits of time ranging in length from five to thirty minutes during your week when you can do something that is related to your creativity. These are called speed-dates.

SPEED-DATES

In your journal brainstorm a list of short activities that you can do in less than thirty minutes. For example:
- *a quick sketch*
- *music practice*

- *sing a song*
- *sand your wood project*
- *be a character and act out their response to various situations, such as hearing sad news or happy news*
- *write playful metaphors on nature.*

Is there something you can do to remind yourself to have creative speed-dates? For example, keep a sketchbook and pencils somewhere you will see them? Perhaps have a list of small things you can do during the week and tick them off as you achieve them? Maybe write yourself a message and stick it on the fridge?

How to get the most out of your creative play-dates and speed-dates

- The first step is to make a commitment to turn up to your date.
- Don't place a high expectation on what you feel you *should* achieve.
- Let yourself play.
- Don't try too hard or be too earnest.
- Trust that in the playing you are moving forward.
- Let go of that Inner Critic.
- Don't play the 'until' game. (I'll tell you more about this game next!)

THE 'UNTIL' GAME

I'm presuming you have the desire to step into your creative world, so don't wait for 'until' to happen.

- I can't write/paint/practise *until* I clean the house/fix

the fence/have coffee with my friend.
- I'll wait *until* I feel in the mood.
- I'll wait *until* I feel less depressed or less anxious.
- I won't get into my novel *until* things have settled down a bit.
- It's not possible to do any enjoyable creative things *until* I have earned enough money.

There are always things happening in life that you can use as 'legitimate' reasons to postpone your creativity. After all, you have to wait *until* they settle! The thing is that once one thing settles another will take its place. So you need to start to make room for this 'calling' of your creative-self now. Perhaps this means letting something go. Even if you start in a small way, start today.

MOTIVATION

Motivation is an interesting experience to unpack. What does it really mean? Perhaps at times you ask yourself questions such as:
- How can I be more motivated?
- Why can't I be more like my sister/friend, who seems so fired up and motivated?

Motivation can be described as having a keen interest in doing something and having faith that you will be successful. It comes from the Latin word for 'movement'. It's about setting ourselves challenging but realistic goals and believing we can achieve them. Therefore we need to *do* something that moves us forward. Naturally we all feel ambivalent from time to time — our motivation will vary.

Internal and external motivation

There are two types of motivation. The first is called intrinsic motivation, which is the keenness you experience from within yourself to be creative. Intrinsic motivators include the drive for satisfaction, enjoyment, interest and the challenge of the creative task. It means you like doing whatever it is for the sake of doing it, rather than being dependent on any outside recognition you may also desire. Artist Barry McCann describes it this way: 'I just love art so much ... I can't really explain the hold it has over me.'

The second type of motivation is called extrinsic motivation and it's the desire to gain recognition from outside yourself. This might start with encouragement from a teacher in a beginner's class to winning a prestigious prize or competition. Extrinsic motivation is valid and desirable in many cases, but first of all we need to have a high level of intrinsic motivation to continue with our creativity. You need to like and want to do what you are doing, although at times you may feel frustrated or discouraged. Naturally, extrinsic motivation provides inspiration. Most of us enjoy the value and appreciation others place on what we create.

Motivation is not a constant experience. It ebbs and flows. Sometimes motivation doesn't start flowing until after we make a start. So don't put things off just because you are not 'in the mood'. Motivation and mood will be stimulated as you express yourself creatively. The questions in the following exercise are useful ones to ask yourself whenever your motivation is low.

MOTIVATING MYSELF

In your journal, answer the following questions:
- *Why do I want to engage in this creative pursuit?*
- *What do I hope to feel in achieving this (satisfaction,*

feeling good about myself)?

- *What do I hope to gain (recognition, appreciation, financial reward)?*
- *What self-talk would help me to keep going with my creative expression?*

CREATIVE TOUCHSTONES

We live in a busy, buzzy world. Often we are swamped with so many things that need our time and attention. This chapter has focused on providing ideas for how you can manage your time on a daily and weekly basis and how to choose pockets of time that can be filled with creative expression. We don't need to wait 'until' our circumstances have changed, we can start *today*, even if only in a small way. We can remember the reason why it's important to keep on going — our internal drive and extrinsic motivation can serve to inspire us ever onward!

Chapter Ten

PROCRASTINATION

I don't wait for moods.
You accomplish nothing if you do that.
Your mind must know it has got to
get down to work.

— PEARL S. BUCK

Procrastination is the art of delay. It's a Latin term that means 'to put off until tomorrow'. When we procrastinate we hope at a superficial level that by ignoring whatever it is we feel we *should* do, it will go away. But you know and I know this doesn't happen. The activity, whether sorting art materials, doing music practice or finishing a project, lurks at the back of our mind. At times it might be briefly forgotten, but it usually scratches away and interferes with the present moment. Perhaps we are trying to have a cup of coffee with a friend or watch television but underneath we know the task is still there waiting to be done! When we think about our creative activity or task we feel guilty, annoyed or anxious. Sound familiar?

Of course, occasionally it's necessary to delay doing something because a genuinely urgent matter needs our attention. However, most of us put things off sometimes, perhaps in one area of our life but not others. For some, procrastination is an entrenched habit that impinges on many areas of life, including creative expression. Whatever degree of procrastination you experience, this chapter will help you to find potent strategies for making changes so that you can attend to your creative life and finish what is ultimately important to you.

The first exercise in this chapter brings out into the open habits that eat away at your time and distract you from your creative expression. Just as we exposed your self-talk in earlier chapters we now need to do the same with procrastination habits. Once they are on the table and looked at with acceptance and even compassion, you are ready to make some changes. So let's start.

PROCRASTINATION HABITS

Here is a list of some of the things people do when they procrastinate. Give some thought to each question (feel free to modify the questions to suit your particular circumstances) and then answer 'Yes', 'No' or 'Sometimes'.

- *Do you put off starting your creative task, waiting for the right moment or mood?*
- *Do you find you have unfinished projects and feel guilty if you start a new one?*
- *Do you find you keep doing easier creative tasks rather than tackle more challenging ones?*
- *Do you find yourself doing other things, e.g. house*

cleaning, making a phone call?
- *Do friends and social opportunities easily distract you?*
- *Do you stare at a blank page/empty canvas rather than making a start?*
- *Do you often work on your project at the last minute in a rushed way?*
- *Do you berate yourself because you haven't given yourself enough time to do the creative task justice? Do you use this as an excuse: 'It's not very good because I didn't have/give it time'?*
- *Do you feel you are letting yourself down, or think of yourself as lazy or hopeless because you don't get around to your creative pursuits as much as you want to?*

Did you acknowledge a habit or two? Before moving on to the next section, write a response to the following two questions about any habits you identified.

1. Look at the questions that provoked either a 'Yes' or 'Sometimes'. Describe the particular ways you go about procrastinating and how you feel when this happens.
2. Are there times when you don't procrastinate? Write about the ways you get into your creative time. Are there thought processes you remember that help you to move on in your creative expression? It's always helpful to acknowledge the positives as we often take them for granted. So think about the exceptions too.

UNDERLYING REASONS FOR PROCRASTINATING

A common myth is that people procrastinate because they are lazy. However, there are several things that can contribute to procrastination, and once these underlying causes are uncovered, procrastination is easier to deal with. Over the years I have found that people who procrastinate often have a noisy Inner Critic who berates them, saying things like, 'You're no good', 'You have no talent', 'You're hopeless/stupid.' As we discussed earlier, the Inner Critic has no faith in your ability and is damaging to self-esteem. There may also be a well-practised Inner Softie who lets you off the hook in some way: 'Don't worry about doing it now. You're too tired/busy [fill in the blank].' Imagine a friend who continually talks to you in these ways. How would you feel? What would you do? Watching television or cleaning the house sounds like a reasonable alternative in an attempt to get away from the negativity offered up by this friend!

We can find strategies to help break our usual pattern of procrastination. However, before finding these strategies, let's look at the reasons we might procrastinate. Understanding our own motivation to behave in certain ways provides the springboard for making changes.

WHY WE PROCRASTINATE

Below is a list of some common reasons why we procrastinate. Read through each point and give yourself a minute or two to think about whether it applies to you. Try not to rush your thinking time.

Self-doubt: *Are you plagued by thoughts that you are not good enough? Do you keep comparing yourself to others? Are you expecting too much of yourself too soon in your creative journey? How noisy are your Inner Critic and Inner Softie?*

Lack of materials and planning: Are you expecting too much of yourself without having adequate materials and time? Have you thought about when to make time for your creative expression?

Fear of making mistakes: Are you driven by perfectionism and get anxious/angry/distressed if you make a mistake and things don't work out as you had hoped? Do you get frustrated easily and then give up?

Loneliness: Do you feel uncomfortable/anxious when you need to spend time alone engaged in your creative pursuit? Do you need to find ways to feel okay in solitude?

Unclear goals: Do you feel overwhelmed by the creative task you want to complete and don't know where to start?

Resistance: Is this something you really want to do or would you rather be doing something else? Is the creative goal yours or someone else's expectation?

Fear of success: Are you afraid of being in the limelight or drawing attention to yourself and what you create? Perhaps you believe that if you are successful you will have to keep it up. Or maybe you have an underlying belief that you don't deserve success. Success can range from finishing a piece of writing for a local competition to more grand success, such as publishing a book.

If you relate to any of the above reasons, write about your experience in your journal or express yourself in some other art form, such as a drawing, painting, poetry or sculpture. Ask yourself, 'When did I first start to think and behave this way? How has this impacted on my life over the years?' As always, be open and non-judgmental. This step in self-awareness is crucial in making helpful changes.

Now you have identified some of the reasons you procrastinate, can you think of what could help? There are many possibilities, such as setting specific goals or dealing with unhelpful self-talk — strategies we have already explored. Before going on to the next section, think of some options. In the next section you'll find lots of ideas to add to the ones you've discovered yourself.

SO WHAT CAN YOU DO?

Procrastination is often linked to low self-esteem, anxiety and depression. Stress levels for procrastinators are much higher than for people who don't procrastinate. However, once we make a start on a task, we tend to feel happier and our stress level starts to drop. There are many strategies to help break our procrastination habits. No one strategy is right for everyone. What's important is a willingness to experiment with different options and work out what's best for you.

In order to break down these strategies we will look at four main stages when people commonly procrastinate:

- Getting organised.
- Deciding on a project you want to do.
- Starting on a project.
- Stopping when the going gets tough.

Let's now look at each stage. I'll ask a number of questions that will help you to identify the areas you need to address in order to move forward.

Getting organised

It's important to have a space or a place for your creativity. Do you need to find somewhere to play your music without worrying about the neighbours? Do you need to find a place in your home to set up your art or craft materials? Do you need to tidy your desk, sort out your studio or workshop?

Does your creative workspace have good ventilation and lighting and an outlook that's inspiring? If you have a dingy workspace, perhaps you can brighten it up in some way so it's a more inviting place in which to be.

And what about materials? Are you using cheap student-quality paint or paper that gives poor results? Do you need more materials and better tools? Do you need to get your piano tuned?

Do you need to find out what workshops, individual tuition and other education is available in your area? Would you like to find a creative buddy or two to work alongside? Do you need to join your local Arts Society? A writers' group? A craft group? Percussion group?

Are you are avoiding creative expression because of your underlying fears? What do you notice your Inner Critic saying about getting ready and making a start? Does your Inner Softie make a comment too? This could be a good time to revisit Chapters Five and Six and the exercises on self-talk and different parts of our personality. Do you use other means to distract yourself, such as alcohol? Are there harmful habits you need to change? It may also help to talk to a counsellor or someone you trust about these things.

Consider your lifestyle. Do you need to engage in certain self-care/stress management strategies discussed in Chapter Seven? Can you identify ways you might waste time, such as watching too much television or spending too much time on social media?

WHAT I NEED TO DO TO GET ORGANISED

What questions in this section hit the mark for you? In your journal write about them and ask yourself:

- *What will I do to set myself up for my creative time?*
- *Am I willing to do this?*
- *What's the first step I need to take?*

Make a commitment and set a time to take this step.

Deciding on a project you want to do

What will I write/paint/sing/play/craft today? This question often causes anxiety especially when asked at the start of your creative time. So it's helpful to think of a few ideas beforehand, as then you will already have a direction in mind. Here are some ways to get you started:

- Generate ideas as you go along in life. Take notice of what you are drawn to and what you are interested in.
- Keep a notebook handy so you can jot down ideas. If you compose music or write poetry, you might become inspired while having coffee in the local café. If you are an artist, take a small pad with you so you can do a quick sketch when inspiration strikes. A camera is helpful too.
- Keep all your ideas. Even though you might not follow through with an idea straightaway, it could be just the inspiration you need later, e.g. ideas for scenes/characters you want to write about/paint/photograph; songs you want to sing; interesting craft projects. Make sure you keep your inspirational material handy, perhaps in a special folder or box so you can look through it when needed. Writing down your ideas also releases the busyness of your mind chatter and helps you to come back to the present moment.

- Keep an art diary or scrapbook for your ideas — you can include pictures from magazines, sayings/words, photos, colours and images.
- Be open to inspiration at different times of the day, whether you are pulling out weeds in your garden or stuck in a traffic jam.
- And finally you don't have to have a specific task in mind when you start your creative time. Start anywhere! You can improvise with sounds or notes, play and experiment with your art materials. Be aware of what emerges when you do this and respond to what evolves. Go with the flow.

Starting on a project

Making a start also daunts many people. There is something challenging about that empty computer screen or blank canvas ... waiting ... waiting. Here are some ideas that can help:

- At the start of your creative time make sure you have all the material and equipment you need. Organise a cup of tea/coffee/water for yourself and whatever else helps you feel ready to go.
- Give yourself permission to start anywhere rather than at the beginning. For example, write the conclusion of your story before the beginning, sing the chorus rather than the verse. This frees you and warms up the creative flow.
- Some people like to create a special ritual as a way to prepare. They feel it helps them to get in the right mood. Perhaps there is certain music you can play. You might like to do a short relaxation and visualisation exercise such as the one described in Chapter Twelve.
- Don't expect yourself to fire up straight away. The mind

and body need to become reacquainted and warmed up before you are ready to create. So give yourself a short warm-up period before the more intensive work begins. If you are an artist, do some simple pencil sketches, dabble with your paints or experiment with little mud maps of your chosen scene. If you are a singer, allow your voice to warm up — perhaps do some improvisation and have some fun. You can also do this if you are a musician or an actor. If you are a writer, you can warm up by reading what you have written previously and brainstorm some ideas about where you might want to go next.

Stopping when the going gets tough

There will be occasions when you are likely to feel challenged and frustrated. Remember that this is part of the creative process. It doesn't mean you haven't got what it takes. Occasionally creative projects go smoothly but sometimes there is challenge after challenge. It's important to accept frustration as part of the process. We can walk away, but this interrupts and halts our progress. Don't resist the challenge and associated feelings; go with it and accept it. See frustration as a chance to ask a different sort of question and search for a new solution. Let the challenge propel you forward. You are likely to be on the brink of something exciting. I know a brilliant leather craftsman who retired to Italy and always had a secret yearning to break into the European market. He needed a particular piece of equipment to stitch his bags in a certain way, but he couldn't find what he needed. It was tough and frustrating. For a long time he searched for another way and finally he came up with something new and innovative that led to his designs selling all over Europe. So don't give up. Keep going! Who knows what you will discover?

What's your usual way?

How we feel and behave when the going gets tough is likely to be similar to how we handle other challenging situations, such as a work problem or conflict with a friend. If our habit is to walk away and avoid frustration or unpleasant feelings then we probably do the same in our creative time too. It's likely our self-talk is something like: 'I can't stand this' or 'This is too difficult', and, as you know from previous chapters, this influences how you feel and what you do. What helps is developing a greater tolerance for these uncomfortable states. At first you can practise accepting frustration and continuing with whatever you are doing for a short period of time, say an extra five minutes. You can practise the centring technique from Chapter Seven and let go of your self-talk that says, 'I can't stand this.' You can affirm yourself by thinking, 'I can do this', and stay with whatever you are doing for another five minutes. This won't harm you. In time you will get used to having a whole range of feelings as you create. They come and go during your creative time. Remind yourself of the value of your creativity.

On the other hand, perhaps you have a tendency to stay and persist no matter what. When the going gets tough, you keep at it like a bull at a gate. Sometimes this is great but at other times you need to learn to walk away from what you are doing for a little while, to have a break so that you can come back with a fresh approach. Perhaps you could go for a quiet walk alone. Or maybe you need to ask for help or at least talk over what is challenging you with someone you trust — maybe a friend, your teacher or fellow artists, writers or performers.

One of the best ways to keep creativity flowing is to do something every day. Depending on your lifestyle this doesn't need to take long. Just a few minutes in addition to your creative play-dates and speed-dates can be valuable. Perhaps a quick line drawing of what's on the kitchen table, singing in the car, jotting down ideas for a wood project or brainstorming some ideas for one of your stories. Don't minimise it by saying it's not valuable. It is. It keeps your creative flow stimulated.

And remember that it's normal to have times of inactivity or low creative energy, especially after completing a project. What's important during these times is to gently accept that this is where you are at. Use the time to fill up your reserves and nourish yourself. There is no doubt your creative mind is still engaged in various ways, but perhaps not as actively or noticeably. And that's fine.

STOPPING PROCRASTINATION

In your journal write down your answers to the following:
- *What did you discover about procrastination?*
- *What's one thing you can change about engaging in your creative pursuit?*
- *What will you **do** about making this change?*

After changing one thing, come back to this chapter and find another strategy to experiment with.

CREATIVE TOUCHSTONES

Procrastination is a habit. It's not laziness. There are reasons why people procrastinate. If you identify with procrastination, I hope you see yourself in a different light now. Rather than judging yourself as weak and lazy, which is demoralising, you can experiment with a whole host of strategies to break the habit. You can take some action, one step at a time and move forward.

Perfectionism is also a reason why people procrastinate and this is what we look at next.

Chapter Eleven

PERFECTIONISM

If you're not prepared to be wrong, you'll never come up with anything original.

— KEN ROBINSON

The quote above is an insightful gem that goes straight *through* the heart of perfectionism. Here's another one from writer Eva Sallis:

'I have this theory that everyone has a layer of crap they have to write through before they get to the good stuff, and the longer you stop writing, the more it just builds up like a sediment, and as soon as you start you've got to write through this rubbish before you get to the good stuff again.'

Phew! What a relief! It's normal to have 'a layer of crap' or rough edges to begin with. This chapter teases out perfectionist tendencies and what's behind this stressful way of being in the world. If you are plagued by perfectionism, you'll find a host of ways to break out of its tight constraints and thus enjoy and move forward in your creative expression.

Just as writers need to 'write through the rubbish', the same principle applies equally to other creative pursuits. If you are an artist, you need the freedom to first paint the ugly ducklings before you paint the swans. If you are a singer, you push the notes at either end of your range and hear the imperfect sounds before you gain mastery. If you are a dancer, you will stumble or go slowly when trying out new steps. If you are learning how to solder, you are likely to first have some uneven joins in your leadlighting or silverware. Unfortunately, perfectionists agonise about going through the 'rubbish' or seeing their ugly ducklings.

Many perfectionists stop themselves from experimenting and playing in their creative discipline because of their impossible standards. However, there is no avoiding imperfection if you want to get ahead in your creative expression. Even professionals make mistakes. They learn to accept and work with them. They learn to keep going. Miranda Otto, a well-known Australian actor, once said, 'I love rehearsing and having time to make mistakes and laugh and discover things about yourself and other people.' A refreshing take on mistakes, don't you think?

HOW TO VIEW MISTAKES

Rather than seeing mistakes as a sign of failure and incompetency, we can learn to see mistakes as an inevitable and rich part of the creative process. In fact, if we are not prepared to make mistakes we won't be creative or achieve originality. We can learn as much from our mistakes as we can from our successes. There are times when your mistakes will surprise you and you will like what you discover. Anyone who has ever painted in watercolours will know the term 'happy accidents'. Something unexpected happens that gives life and originality to the painting. This can happen in any creative discipline, so allow yourself to make mistakes as you learn.

Perfectionism stifles freedom and without freedom there is no creativity. Most importantly, perfectionism takes away our pleasure and joy. The other day I was watching the television program *So You Think You Can Dance*. One particular dancer was perfect, but he kept getting feedback that he wasn't connecting to the audience. He was so caught up in technical perfection that he failed to convey his essence as a performer. This failure tainted his 'perfect' performance and left him seeming rather cold and mechanical. On a less grand scale I remember that when I first started to paint I would try to do it very carefully. I found it quite stressful and the end result looked like a painting by numbers: stiff and lacking expression. Now, I take great pleasure in leaving the juicy marks of a wet paintbrush.

THE INJURIES OF PERFECTIONISM

There is a significant difference between taking pleasure and pride in striving to accomplish something to the best of your ability and pushing yourself to reach unrealistic standards. These standards are usually self-prescribed and are reinforced by our perception of what we believe other people expect from us. Perfectionists don't enjoy the process of their creativity because they are so focused on the perfect end result they believe they must achieve. Another unfortunate feature of perfectionism is that it's often associated with stress and anxiety that inevitably interfere with what you are doing.

DO YOU IDENTIFY WITH PERFECTIONISM?

If you are not sure whether or not you're a perfectionist, try this quick quiz. Read the following statements indicating some different ways perfectionists think and behave. Answer how each statement applies to you with a 'Yes', 'No' or 'Sometimes'.

- *I can never seem to finish a drawing/painting/writing/ project.*
- *I keep rewriting the same sentence/paragraph time and time again, but it never seems right.*
- *I keep playing/singing the same tune/song time and time again trying to get it right, but it never feels right.*
- *I never feel satisfied and feel I have to keep practising/ writing/working on my project. It never feels 'good enough'.*
- *I keep comparing myself to others and feel I can never get to their standard.*
- *I never seem to meet the standards I set for myself.*
- *I think mistakes mean that I am not 'good enough'.*
- *I'm afraid that others will see my flaws and judge me.*
- *If someone saw a mistake I'd made I'd feel humiliated.*

How did you go? If you said 'Yes' to several of these statements, it's likely that perfectionism is impacting on your creative time. If you answered 'Sometimes' to several of these statements then obviously it's less of a problem and there are times when you resist being driven by perfectionism. I wonder what helps you to resist on these occasions?

WAYS OF BEING A PERFECTIONIST

Perfectionists generally have two main ways of behaving. Either they work very hard and for long hours endeavouring to meet their impossible standards, or they avoid the task and experience the negative consequences of procrastination that we looked at in the last chapter.

Perfectionists who work long hours are pedantic about the smallest details. They are often successful and receive positive feedback from others. Unfortunately, this reinforces their belief that they must continue to work this way. However, there is a price to pay because perfectionists are usually very stressed and tense and they often sacrifice other important areas of their life in pursuit of their perfectionism. Let me tell you about Karla.

KARLA

Karla is a talented graphic designer who works a fourteen-hour day and neglects her social life and health. She works painstakingly, taking about three times longer to achieve results similar to those of her colleagues. She never feels her current project is finished. Her colleagues receive positive feedback too, but they have the benefit of a full and rounded life.

To help Karla move forward she takes an honest look at the pros and cons of working this way, so as to see in black and white, on paper, the effect of perfectionism on her life. This is what she discovers when she looks at the consequences of her behaviour.

Advantages: I get terrific feedback from the boss, who keeps telling me she appreciates my commitment. My clients are always satisfied. One year I got a Staff Award and I hope to again. Mum and Dad continue to be proud of me. Mostly I avoid getting criticised.

Disadvantages: My health is suffering — I'm putting on weight and feel very unfit. I feel lonely — I never have time to go out. My workmates are starting to avoid me because I never have time to chat. I feel continually anxious during the week. Sometimes when I slow down on the weekends I feel dull and depressed. I'm wondering if this is all there is to life. Sometimes I do get criticised, even though I have tried so hard to get it right.
I feel dreadful.

It's important for Karla to be upfront and acknowledge how her behaviour is affecting her. By seeing the number of negatives written down, she starts to think about what she can do differently. Although she is quite fearful, she starts by reducing the number of hours she stays in the office and restricts the amount of time she spends on each project. She chooses an easy project to begin with, so she can practise limiting her time and not being so pedantic. She finds it challenging and needs to practise some centring (Chapter Seven) and helpful self-talk to guide herself through (Chapter Five). She enlists both her Inner Supporter and Inner Guide (Chapter Six). When she completes a small project in this new way she feels encouraged to take the same approach to other projects. She starts having faith in her ability to do things differently. It's not easy or comfortable for Karla to make these changes and sometimes she finds herself slipping into her old ways. Nevertheless she keeps practising. Slowly she realises that cutting down the time for each project has very little effect on the outcome or feedback she receives. She also notices her mood improves by going home early and taking a walk.

ADVANTAGES AND DISADVANTAGES OF PERFECTIONISM

If you identify with aspects of perfectionism here is a helpful exercise. In your journal divide your page in half so you can list advantages on one side and disadvantages on the other. Write down as many advantages and disadvantages to thinking and behaving this way as you can. What do you discover? Is your list of disadvantages longer than your list of advantages?

Perfectionism and self-worth

What is soul destroying for perfectionists is that they measure their worth in terms of their ability to meet their incredibly high standards. Underneath, perfectionists believe they are not good enough and they have a tyrannical Inner Critic that attempts to whip them into perfect shape. You can see how Karla ties her self-worth to her achievements rather than accepting herself as a worthwhile and capable person.

WHERE DOES PERFECTIONISM COME FROM?

Perhaps you discovered the answer to this question when you read Chapter Three. It may be that perfectionism was role-modelled by someone significant in your early life. Quite possibly you witnessed a parent being pedantic in areas such as housework, their diet or how they did their job. Maybe they gave you lots of rules — 'shoulds' and 'musts' on how to get on in the world. Or perhaps you were bright and creative as a child and your parents always very positively rewarded anything outstanding. This is not a bad thing, but sometimes a child comes to the conclusion that they are only okay if they don't make mistakes. Or perhaps you were only loved if you were seen to be smart. On the other hand you might have been punished for making mistakes and quickly learnt to do everything you could to avoid this. You might have been a carefree child, but certain teachers scolded and moulded you to conform to their tight constraints of being a 'good' or perfect pupil.

Perfectionism doesn't have to come from your childhood. It could be that at some stage in your work or creative life you experienced a couple of surprising early successes. It may be that this conditioned your future behaviour to continue to strive to get things perfect.

The different ways perfectionists think

Perfectionists have ways of thinking that keep them locked into their drive to be flawless. These ways are unrealistic and certainly unhelpful. Their Inner Critic is very active. Let's look at some common examples.

Many perfectionists engage in *all-or-nothing thinking* about the excessively high standards they believe they *must* achieve. Tom says, 'If I don't win a prize in the poetry competition it means my writing is no good.'

Perfectionists often *overgeneralise*. Jane forgot to spray her charcoal drawing with fixative and says to herself, 'I always goof up. I'm never going to be the artist I want to be.' You can see how words such as 'always' and 'never' are extreme and inaccurate. These words diminish her self-esteem and faith in her ability.

Many perfectionists also engage in *catastrophic thinking*. They tell themselves that something awful will happen if things don't work out the way they want: 'I must get the part in the play or else my life as an actor is over.' Perfectionists often use words like 'must' and 'should'.

Filtering is another way of thinking. It's a tendency to focus and *magnify negative details* at the expense of the positive. When we filter we are being selective and only giving attention to people and events that confirm our belief system. For example, if you learnt as a child that your artistic creativity is not as important as getting a 'decent' job and high income, you are likely to notice things that confirm your beliefs. So you tend to notice 'poor' artists rather than the successful ones.

Perfectionists are also adept at *comparing* themselves to others. Someone is always smarter and more talented. They overlook their own strengths and unique abilities.

Perfectionists often keep themselves locked into thinking that their creative piece is *never finished* and that there is always more work to be done. It's important to accept that the song, the painting, the piece of writing or project may never be 'finished', because we can always continue to change or edit what we have produced. However, for each piece of creative work there comes a time when we need to say, 'That's it!' and move on.

IMPERFECT THINKING PATTERNS

Do you identify with any of the above ways of thinking? Do you find they influence your approach to your creative time?

If you do, write them down in your journal. Don't let them float around in your head depleting your creative energy. See them in black and white, for what they are: your Inner Critic taking control. Now would be a good time to go back to the exercises in Chapters Five and Six on changing self-talk and enlisting the help of your Inner Supporter and Inner Guide.

ANTIDOTES TO PERFECTIONISM

Perfectionism stifles creativity because the very essence of creativity is the freedom to think and play expansively. We need to experiment in lots of ways in order to find what we like or don't like and what works well or doesn't work well. One way to combat perfectionism is to decide on some experimental projects to help you resist getting things perfect. The aim of these projects is to practise feeling free and not worry about the end result. I say 'practise' because you will most likely find it a challenge and it will take time for you to get used to approaching your creativity in this way. Here are some ideas to play with.

- Paint a painting in half an hour.
- Write a short story in an hour.
- Sing something out of your usual range.
- Paint on cardboard rather than a canvas.
- Act out a character and deliberately be over the top.
- Dance to music you don't like.
- Write a song in half an hour.
- Draw in pen you can't rub out.
- Close your eyes and mould clay for ten minutes.

- Attempt to express an emotion.
- Design some 'crazy' craft projects.
- Deliberately mould an unattractive pot.

Can you think of some other challenges for yourself?

PRACTISE IMPERFECTION

Choose one of the above exercises or one you have designed yourself and practise being imperfect! Afterwards, write about your experience by answering the following four questions:

- *What did I like about doing this exercise?*
- *What didn't I like?*
- *What have I learnt from doing this exercise?*
- *What's the worst that can happen if/when I don't like the end result?*

CREATIVE TOUCHSTONES

Perfectionism in its purest form is a torment. As it attempts to whip you into perfect shape it drains from you the energy you need to be the best you can. How you think and what you continue to *do* will propel perfectionism to take away the joy in your life. Like procrastination, there are many habits that contribute to perfectionism that can be challenged and changed. This chapter has focused on understanding the torment and provided strategies to help break this habit. Above all, perfectionism is the antithesis of creativity, as it takes away our capacity to play. And to play is the secret of true creativity.

Chapter Twelve

CREATIVE MINDFULNESS

You can't stop the waves,
but you can learn to surf.

— JON KABAT-ZINN

Throughout this book compassionate self-knowledge has been the foundation of our creative story. Self-knowledge enables us to celebrate our strengths and provides the impetus to make changes to the thoughts and behaviours that thwart creative expression. This chapter offers another empowering tool called mindfulness — a practice that enriches our creative expression by connecting us to the here and now.

MINDFULNESS

Mindfulness is intentionally paying attention to the present moment in a calm and non-judgmental way. We avoid judging the present moment as good or bad, whether we are watching a beautiful sunset or experiencing a headache. We notice and gently accept each experience as it unfolds, moment by moment. We pay attention to what we perceive through our senses of hearing, smelling, tasting, seeing and touch. We have a friendly attitude towards our experience and ourselves. When we are mindful we are not caught up in the past or worrying about the future.

Imagine being totally focused on and engaged in what you are doing in all parts of your life: talking to the family, playing golf, making love, listening to a friend, painting, drawing, singing, knitting, dancing or whatever you enjoy. Even with unpleasant experiences, such as a headache or distressing feelings, mindfulness helps us to compassionately accept our experience rather than add unhelpful thoughts and tension. We can practise mindfulness at any time. You can have a go right now. Stop for a moment and do this short exercise. You'll need to pause throughout the exercise to allow time for each suggestion.

PRACTISING MINDFULNESS

Just sit and be still. What are you aware of right now? Let your mind drift to whatever comes into your consciousness. Be a friendly and curious observer ... Are you aware of sounds around you? Let your mind drift from one sound to the next ... Or perhaps you notice the silence ... Notice when a thought comes into your mind ... Notice each thought and gently let it go ... Are you aware of any physical sensations? ... Bring your attention to your feet ... Feel the sensation of your feet supported by the floor ... Just notice these sensations ... What other physical sensations can you notice right now? ... Maybe you notice something unpleasant, like some muscle tension ... Observe if you judge this in some way ... Just notice and be aware of the sensations and let go of any thoughts or judgments about your experience ... Gently let your mind

scan your body ... Be aware of sensations inside or outside
your body ... And then, when you are ready, move on to
something else that you notice ... If it helps, you can think to
yourself, 'Now I'm aware of ... now I'm aware of ...'

If this is your first conscious attempt at mindfulness, don't be discouraged if you became distracted. I use the word 'conscious' because there are times in your life when you are mindful without actually giving the experience the label of mindfulness. These are the occasions when you are focused and absorbed in the present — maybe listening to your favourite piece of music or experiencing the cool breeze from a fan on a hot day as it touches your skin. Mindfulness sounds deceptively simple but it's not easy to begin with. Imagine your mind like a road map with different tracks running all over it. We constantly travel from one track to the next and then to the next. One minute we are thinking about a news item, the next minute feeling annoyed about the surly shop assistant we met in the supermarket and then worrying about our finances. Busy, busy, busy mind. This happens to us all. It's normal. Our mind chatters about all sorts of things that can take us away from being connected to the present. Some of these thoughts are particularly unhelpful and discouraging, as we have discovered in previous chapters. We are often bombarded by external stimuli too: traffic, phone, computer, television, radio. However, we *can* learn how to stand back from external stimuli and our busy mind so they don't cloud our present experience.

The next exercise gives you the opportunity to practise mindfulness in your daily life. By practising mindfulness during everyday experiences you will find it easier to bring mindfulness to your creative life.

EVERYDAY MINDFULNESS

In this exercise you are asked to heighten your awareness of a familiar experience. For each suggested experience remember three important steps:

1. *Be attentive to the present moment in a friendly and curious way.*
2. *Notice distractions and gently let them go.*
3. *Come back to your present experience.*

Mindfully have your shower. Be aware of the water as it streams down your skin, the sound of the water, the slippery feel of the soap as it moves over your body, the texture of the towel as you dry yourself.

Mindfully eat a meal without the television, radio or newspaper. Carefully pay attention to the food on your plate. Notice the colours ... sense the smells ... notice how you cut the food and then notice the sensation of taking the food to your mouth ... experience the sensation of chewing ... and the sensation of swallowing. You may only be able to do this for a few moments before you become distracted; that's okay. Gently notice that you are distracted. Let go of any thoughts of evaluation as you do this exercise.

Here are some other ideas:

- *Mindfully do a chore such as making your bed or mowing the lawn.*
- *Look at and immerse yourself in a beautiful sunset.*
- *Pat your dog and notice the sensations of the experience.*
- *Feel the refreshment of cold water on a hot day.*

We can practise mindfulness at any time of the day or in any situation. Pushing a shopping trolley through the car park might seem mundane but it can take on a different texture when you are with the experience completely. Start practising mindfulness for a few minutes a day or even for thirty seconds several times a day.

MINDFUL OBSERVATION

As you can see, mindfulness enhances your ability to be tuned in to everyday life. This has a direct benefit to creativity. By being present centred you take in the richness of life around you, which becomes the fodder for your creative expression. Mindfulness is sometimes called 'beginner's mind' because you look at something as if for the first time. You regard the world with childlike wonder. Mindfulness helps you to become in tune: in tune with nature, with your feelings and within your relationships. You are open and curious. In this way, mindfulness helps you to build a rich reservoir of memories and material for your creative work. If you are an artist, imagine mindfully taking in the shapes, colours and nuances of your landscape and environment as you go for a walk.

Regardless of your creative discipline, you can become more attentive or mindful during a whole host of creative situations. Let's look at a few.

Mindful music

Mindfully listen to music you enjoy. Listen to the sounds as they unfold. Just listen. Notice any feelings that emerge ... no evaluation, no judgment. Just hear the sounds and experience whatever comes into your awareness. If you become distracted, simply notice that your mind has wandered and come back to listening to the music. First, try listening to soothing, slow-paced music and then, at another time, listen to music that is energetic and uplifting. Try being mindful of one instrument at a time. For example, follow the sounds of the piano or the oboe. Discover the delightful nuances of each instrument as you listen in this way.

Mindful reading

Silently read a piece of writing you like. Read it slowly and deliberately. Hear the sound that each word makes. Now try reading the same piece of writing out loud and listen to the sounds, notice the rhythms and gently feel the meaning of the words as you read.

Mindful objects

Find an object that you would like to touch — a ceramic pot, a woven rug, the bark of a tree. Slowly feel the object and notice each sensation as it unfolds. Just notice ... no evaluation, no judgment. Besides your sense of touch, the senses of sight, smell and even taste may be stimulated.

Mindful art

Look at a painting. What do you see? Rather than giving names to what is in the painting, such as a tree or sky, notice the colours, the shapes, the contours, the lights and the darks, the diagonals and the verticals, the negative shapes and the positive shapes. Notice whether any feelings emerge as you look at the painting. After mindfully observing the painting, close your eyes and let go of the image. Become aware of your feelings and what emerges from your subconscious.

MINDFULNESS OF THOUGHTS

Another benefit of mindfulness practice is that it helps you to have a different relationship to unhelpful thoughts. Rather than thoughts controlling you, you find you have ways to manage them so they don't deplete, depress or demotivate you. Even if your thoughts are 'stubborn', mindfulness helps to turn down their volume as if you were adjusting the sound on your radio or device. Noticing a thought such as, 'My writing is awful' gives you the opportunity to simply let it go, without adding extra self-criticism and turning it into a huge ball of negativity. To notice and name what is happening and then let it go frees up your creative energy. Mindfulness helps you to *be* in the present, which helps you to *do* your creative task. Let's see how mindfulness helped Mia.

MIA

Mia is a bright and lively creative dance student. She loves to dance freely and choreograph routines for a dance troupe she is in, but she often feels depleted and discouraged despite high praise from others. She is aware of an Inner Critic that picks away quietly and consistently at her efforts: 'This has been done before', 'The others won't like this', etc. She has tried to be more positive and sometimes it really helps to give herself encouragement — 'This is great!', 'I like this new move!' — but at other times it seems more difficult. At these times she finds it helpful to switch on her mindfulness. (Remember that this is deliberately paying attention to what's going on in the present moment in a non-judgmental way.) Mia thinks to herself, 'Oh yes, I know what's happening; I'm listening to that "stuff" inside my head which isn't helpful at all. I'm going to let it go and focus on this new routine.' She begins by bringing her attention to her breathing and experiencing each step of her routine as it unfolds. She listens to the rhythm and vibration of the music as it sinks into her being and stimulates her movement. She then finds she is able to get into the zone of her dancing.

Getting into the zone of our creativity has been described as 'flow'. You lose your self-consciousness and become absorbed in what you are doing. Time often seems to stand still. Practising mindfulness helps you to achieve this flow. When you learn to quieten your mind you create more space for creative impulses, thoughts and expression. But remember, this takes practice.

CREATING IN THE NOW

Just as for Mia, there will be times during our creative expression when we are distracted. When we are not in the moment of what we are doing. When we are thinking of something else or trying to do two things at the same time. Maybe we are worried about something or simply thinking about what's happening in the world. It's normal. However, we need to become conscious that this is what we are doing. As we become conscious of our distracted mind, we move into being mindful — mindful of our thoughts, just as Mia did in the example. We are then able to shift our attention back to what we are doing. Consider the following suggestions as ways to practise mindfulness to stimulate creativity. This is part of the experimental phase of the SEED process, and also gives you the opportunity to develop skills.

Writing mindfully

Remember that mindfulness means having a beginner's mind and thus having a childlike wonder and curiosity about what unfolds. So give yourself some time to write freely and spontaneously and let the words flow. Allow words and phrases to bubble up into your consciousness and write them down. Allow yourself to be aware of whatever arises with an attitude of non-judgment. You can start with giving yourself ten minutes and then build up to thirty minutes or longer. You need not look at this writing again; just let it be an exercise in mindfulness. Alternatively, you can read it mindfully and tune in to your feelings and see what inspires you, perhaps for your next poem or story.

Try the same approach for specific topics. For example, write about:

- a child playing
- an old woman embracing a cat
- a thunderstorm.

Remember: no judgment or evaluation. This writing is in the experimental phase of the SEED approach. At another stage you can begin the process of evaluating and editing.

Drawing and painting mindfully

Without a topic in mind allow yourself to draw or paint whatever comes into your consciousness. This is not about making a work of art, but rather giving yourself permission to be uninhibited and experience the unfolding of lines, strokes, colours and shapes as they emerge. Remember to do this mindfully, so be fully aware of your experience rather than proceeding on automatic pilot. This exercise is similar to doodling, but with attentive awareness of what unfolds.

At another time choose a topic, such as landscapes or portraits, and see what emerges.

When looking at an object or scene for a drawing or painting, take your time and be attentive to all the nuances of what you see and feel. Let go of any preconceptions of what you think something looks like. Consider the foreshortening that occurs when viewing a reclining figure feet first. What we see are huge feet, a truncated body and a small head. Instead of thinking we must draw the body bigger than the feet (which it is in life), we let go of our preconceptions and deliberately and carefully notice the lines, distances and shapes that will help us to achieve accuracy in our portrayal of the figure.

Singing and playing music mindfully

When on your own, warm up by singing or playing any notes that freely and naturally arise. Next, move on to singing your song or playing your piece of music mindfully. Listen to the sounds as they unfold. Singing or playing in this way means you are able to let go of distractions and allow yourself to be in touch with the emotion of the piece of music and/or lyrics.

Listening mindfully helps you to notice if you are rushing certain parts, or perhaps singing or playing too softly or too loudly. Of course what is important here is that you become aware without negative judgment. You are merely becoming attentive to your musical experience and, if you choose, you can change your approach next time.

When singing or playing music with others, practise fully extending your awareness to what you hear all around you. You probably do this already, but now *consciously* extend your attentiveness to your fellow singers or musicians. This is not about concentrating harder, but about opening your awareness to what is 'sounding' around you.

Acting mindfully

Tell a story about something that has happened to you recently and tell it in the present tense. Leave out the word 'and' to help your storytelling be fresh and immediate. We often overuse the word 'and', which tends to dilute the energy of the story and makes us waffle. I remember the fun of playing this game with the kids in the car on long journeys! As you tell your story notice how you feel, notice any hesitations and if there is any background commentary in your mind about what you are saying.

Pretend to be a character in your novel or play and tell a story in the present tense. This story does not need to be the actual story of the play or novel, but it can be something additional that helps you step into the character's shoes in a present moment.

Mindful photography

Look at the object you want to photograph. Take your time and give your full attention to your visual and emotional response. Let go of naming the specifics of what you see, but rather notice the shapes, colours, light and the other nuances of your scene. Notice the foreground and the background. Listen to how you respond internally before you take your photograph.

Sculpting mindfully

Take a lump of clay and give yourself time to notice how it feels as you hold it. Tune in to how the clay feels as you mould and shape it. Feel the weight of the clay, the texture. Do you notice a smell? Stay mindful as you keep exploring and moulding the clay as you shape it into different forms.

It's possible that I haven't specifically mentioned your creative interest in this chapter, but I hope you have gathered enough information and experimented with mindfulness in everyday life so that you can understand and experience the richness that mindfulness can give you. Whatever your creative interest, practise mindfulness and notice the difference! Write about your experiences in your journal and, above all, be present.

CREATIVE TOUCHSTONES

Mindfulness is simply about being intentionally aware of the present moment in an open and gentle way. Mindfulness shifts us away from our preoccupations and worries and transports us into the aliveness of the now. This aliveness feeds our creative energy and opens up the rich and colourful world around us. Although mindfulness is a natural state of being, we are continually drawn away from this state because of the busy, noisy world we live in. The deliberate practice of mindfulness helps to re-establish this natural state of being. Solitude and silence help too, and this is what we explore in the final chapter.

Chapter Thirteen

SOLITUDE, SILENCE AND SPIRITUALITY

When I am … completely myself, entirely alone … or during the night when I cannot sleep, it is on such occasions that my ideas flow best and most abundantly. Whence and how these ideas come I know not nor can I force them.

— WOLFGANG AMADEUS MOZART

Aldous Huxley once said, 'The twentieth century is, among other things the Age of Noise.' Now, in the twenty-first century, with the additional growth of technology, we are constantly surrounded by and tempted to engage in newer forms of technological development. Technology can accompany us everywhere. For many, even waiting at the bus stop is filled with the activity of a mobile device: surfing the net, checking emails or talking to someone.

What part does silence and solitude play in your creative life?

You may find the idea of solitude and silence quite daunting or perhaps you already enjoy time alone to play and create or simply appreciate the quiet. How can we nurture solitude and silence, especially if it feels alien? And what about spirituality? For many people their spirituality is intimately linked to their creativity. This spirituality need not be religious, but rather a deep connection to what is inspiring and meaningful in our lives.

THE VALUE OF SOLITUDE

Solitude is not the same as loneliness. When we are lonely we feel isolated and bereft of human company. Solitude, on the other hand, means intentionally giving ourselves time to be alone; to be free from the usual distractions and demands in our life. We give ourselves time to just *be* who we are. We can also take the opportunity to reflect on our lives.

Solitude creates a 'space' for creative ideas to surface. It also provides a time for creative daydreaming; a time to be introspective, to ponder and play in our imagination. Solitude gives us time to practise and experiment creatively without the demands of the outside world. Choosing deliberate periods of solitude does not diminish the value of the stimulation and support we find with others. It just provides the opportunity for a different, introspective stimulus for our creativity.

THE CHALLENGE OF SOLITUDE

How do you feel about having time on your own? Do you feel you must keep busy and spend most of your time with others? Are you aware of the amount of time you spend in front of the television, computer and other mobile devices? Sometimes our busyness covers underlying fears. But, as we have discovered, it's better for our worries and fears to come to the surface and be dealt with, rather than simmer below our consciousness and zap our creative energy.

PRACTISING SOLITUDE

If you already enjoy solitude, give yourself some time to reflect in your journal on what you appreciate about being on your own and the benefits you experience, especially creative benefits.

But if you haven't given solitude much thought before or are even somewhat afraid of the idea, here are some ways to begin practising being on your own. I say 'practising', because being on your own may feel unusual and it might take time to relish the gifts of solitude.

- *Walk on your own without the distraction of a mobile device.*
- *Enjoy the peace and quiet of soaking in a bath.*
- *Take ten minutes to sit in your garden or in a park and just be aware of your surroundings.*
- *Deliberately set aside some time when you don't turn on the radio, television or other electronic device.*
- *Resist listening to the radio or music when you are driving on your own. Stop and park somewhere for a while and experience the bubble of solitude.*
- *Ride a bike and feel the freedom of being on your own.*
- *Try out the mindfulness exercises in the previous chapter.*
- *Work up to spending several hours on your own, and then a day or a whole weekend.*

When you practise solitude, don't try to make things happen.

Don't put pressure on yourself to come up with creative ideas. Allow them to emerge. Remember all the skills you have learnt in previous chapters.

SILENCE THROUGH MEDITATION

Daily meditation practice gives you the time for short periods of solitude and silence in a busy day. Meditation is also another way of being mindful and helps us to let go of the clutter in our minds. We take our attention away from our everyday thoughts and come back to the present moment. When we learn to gently silence the busyness of our mind, we become more in tune with our inner creative essence.

In meditation you focus your mind on one thing, often called the object of attention, while letting go of distractions. As you practise meditation you develop a mental 'muscle' to help you stay in the here and now. In your mind you create a new pathway that isn't full of busyness and worry. Research has shown increased plasticity of the brain in response to any repetitive practice such as meditation. We have the ability to create new neurons and to quieten down old 'unhelpful' ones that have formed a track in our minds. Meditation interrupts the pattern of an old pathway and creates a new one. It is as healthy for the mind as exercise is for the body.

How to meditate

There are many meditation traditions across cultures, including movement meditations such as Tai Chi Chuan and Qigong, using prayer beads such as the rosary in the Catholic Church, and the Koan riddle in Japanese culture. Many meditation practices, such as within Buddhism, focus on awareness of the breath and this is what I suggest in the next exercise. In other traditions people use a word or sound called a mantra that they silently repeat as a way to help them stay focused — a word such as 'peace' or 'calm' or even counting from one to four. Others silently say 'breathing in' with the inward breath and 'breathing out' with the outward breath. Although there are lots of ways to meditate it's important to stay with whatever 'object of attention' you choose rather than to keep trying different ones. What inevitably happens in the practice of meditation is that you notice your mind strays to different thoughts and other distractions such as sounds or physical sensations. This is normal and a natural part of meditation. You simply notice this is happening in a gentle and non-judgmental way and then come back to your focus. You do this time and time again. With practice, you learn to go into a quieter, deeper place within yourself. It's like looking at a cloudy sky, where you have layers of clouds (busy thoughts), but with practice you move into the quiet surrender of the blue sky beyond the clouds. Meditation facilitates a deep connection to your inner creative-self.

I suggest that you begin with five to ten minutes a day and gradually build up to fifteen to thirty minutes. It's beneficial to begin with a short daily practice rather than a longer practice once a week. Success in a small goal will encourage you to keep going.

MEDITATION PRACTICE

Find a quiet place where you won't be interrupted. You might like to create a space in your home that is inspiring for meditation. Perhaps place a beautiful cloth on a small table, light a candle, have a flower in a vase or some other symbol that is meaningful to you.

Take off your shoes and loosen any tight clothing.

Sit in a chair that supports your back in an upright position (unless you are comfortable sitting cross-legged on the floor on a cushion).

Place your hands in your lap and have both feet supported by the floor or, if you sit on a cushion, have your knees resting on the floor on another lower cushion.

Gently close your eyes. Allow your body to relax — especially your jaw, shoulders, belly and hands.

Take a few minutes to scan your body from head to toe. If you notice any tension gently breathe in and out as if from this part of your body.

Now allow your mind to focus on your breath (or a mantra if you prefer), either the sensation of the breath as it moves in and out of the nostrils or the rise and fall of your abdomen. When thoughts or distractions enter your mind, just notice this happening, let go and gently come back to your focus. You will do this time and time again in your meditation.

At the end of your practice, slowly open your eyes and sit quietly for a minute or two. Enjoy the sense of peace and calm.

I have taught meditation for many years and witnessed the benefits unfold for people faithful to their practice. As you practise meditation you may find that creative ideas rise to the surface of your mind. This can be exciting and quite seductive and you might be tempted to follow your creative ideas during your meditation practice. But if you do, you stop meditating. So practise letting go of these seductive, creative thoughts and give yourself some time after meditation to write them down. Keep a notebook close by, but don't put too much pressure on yourself to remember your creative ideas. Trust that they will emerge again.

CREATIVITY AS YOU SLEEP

Ideas and solutions to creative problems are sometimes revealed during sleep. This is a time when our mind is relaxed and we seem to be able to sift through a mass of knowledge and information and make links that are sometimes difficult to find in a waking state. Similarly, in the morning when we are in that dreamy, drowsy state, creative ideas can emerge. The key is to not try to make it happen. Just relax and be aware of what comes to the surface of your mind after a good night's sleep. You might be delighted! Again, a nearby notebook can be handy.

CREATIVE VISUALISATION

Most of us lead very busy lives. We often rush from one thing to the next and sometimes it can be hard to settle into our creative space. Our creative time arrives but our mind feels preoccupied with thoughts about different things we have been doing and what still needs to be done. These may not be worrying or negative thoughts, but just those of a busy mind. Taking a few minutes to still our mind and to settle the firing of all those brain neurons is beneficial in creating a mind space for creativity. A few minutes of meditation or using the centring technique described in Chapter Seven is beneficial. You can also add the following visualisation.

VISUALISATION PRACTICE

After quietly watching your breath for a few minutes, gently allow yourself to think about your creative time about to begin. Ask yourself, 'What's important for me today? What do I most wish for? Is there a particular goal?' If so, allow yourself to picture your goal ... Perhaps you can see in your mind's eye what you want to achieve in the session ... words on a page ... a painting on a canvas ... accomplishment in whatever performance activity you engage in ... Or perhaps you most desire a sense of freedom to explore ... Imagine that you are feeling centred and confident ... Picture yourself at the end of your session and the look of satisfaction and pleasure on your face ... acceptance of what you have done. If difficult thoughts come up, just notice them ... perhaps even label them 'unhelpful thoughts'. Be gentle and non-judgmental towards these thoughts ... just let them go ... and come back to the present. At this time you might like to give yourself an affirmation to support your creative process ... perhaps something like, 'I am free to express myself ... I can do this.'

SPIRITUALITY AND CREATIVITY

The word spirit comes from the Latin *spiritus* meaning 'breath', 'breath of God' or 'inspiration'. Words such as 'spirit' and 'spirituality' conjure up different images for different people. Spirituality may resonate as being an integral part of your life or you may not relate to spirituality at all. Just take from this section whatever you connect with.

So what might we mean by spirituality? I like the way health professionals Ruth Murray and Judith Zentner describe it in this broad and inclusive way: 'A quality that goes beyond religious affiliation, that strives for inspiration, reverence, awe, meaning and purpose, even in those who do not believe in God.' Some people experience reverence and awe within the bounds of nature: sitting on a hilltop overlooking magnificent valleys or walking along the beach watching the pounding of the waves as they roll onto shore. Other people find their spiritual self is nurtured within a church or a group of like-minded people.

We hear people say, 'That's the spirit!' — an encouragement, an acknowledgment of a 'sparky' way of being in the world or dealing with a situation. But it may also suggest something deep within the person with which they connect. It's intangible, mysterious and hard to describe.

The transformative nature of creativity

In both spirituality and creativity there is something that is beyond the everyday experience of the self, where one is transcending the ordinary and expected sense of self. There is a sense of mystery at the heart of both creativity and spirituality, despite the logical processes you have been offered in this book. When connected to our spirituality and creativity we experience a heightened sense of consciousness. We are tuned in to our senses — sight, hearing, smell, touch, taste and intuition. When we are in full flight, our creative expression takes us beyond what we first imagined. A transformation occurs. We do not so much *change* as rather become *more* of who we already are. We give form and expression to our inner potential. We often have a desire to express this deepest part of ourselves. With this expression there comes a sense of purpose and when something is meaningful it fuels our passion. We begin to love what we do and keep doing it because we are connected to something deep within. The expression of something that is significant to us is likely to evoke an equally deep response in the viewer or listener.

EXPLORING SPIRITUALITY

Spirituality is deeply connected to such existential questions as:

- *Who am I?*
- *What is my purpose?*
- *What is it that I love to do?*
- *What gives meaning to my life?*
- *How does my creative expression give meaning to my life?*

Ponder on these questions and give yourself time to explore the answers in your journal.

CREATIVE TOUCHSTONES

By giving yourself time to just be who you are away from the noise and busyness of the world you provide space for your unique creativity to unfold. Solitude and silence nourish your deep inner creative ideas and urges. Meditation is a time-honoured practice that teaches us how to be silent and experience solitude. Being present centred, whether in meditation, daily life or sitting by a river, is a powerful avenue to connect to the transformative power of your inner creative spirit.

A final note

Throughout this book, I have emphasised the nature of creative expression as a journey you take in steps. These are not necessarily linear steps because you often come back to a place where you have been before, although enriched by whatever creative experience you have given time to.

Creativity is open to us all. It is not something you either have or don't have. But you do need to start with a small desire to explore something new. It takes courage to accept the ugly ducklings, whether they are words on a page, notes you sing or play, landscapes you paint or roughcast sculptures.

By developing a compassionate stance in all you do and using the strategies in this book you can't help but move forward. So don't give up. And if you happen to give up for a while, come back to what you know deep inside is your creative spark that needs nurturing.

Many of you are already established on this road of your creative life. I hope the strategies offered in this book help you to deal with the inevitable challenges that come your way. My own experience of developing my artistic abilities over the past decade or so has been truly fascinating. If only you could see those first drawings and paintings! Of course I have a long way to go, but I am where I want to be and doing what gives me life.

May you and I continue to enjoy and celebrate our unique creative gifts.

Acknowledgments

My heartfelt thanks to Su Dorland, Brian Connor, Linda Turner, Lynne Hosking, Tess McCallum, Jane O'Sullivan and Margaret Hadfield, all of whom gave their time to read, offer astute advice and thoughtful encouragement. And to Eleanor Dawson for nurturing my creative spirit.

In particular, I thank my partner Graeme, for his patience, support, wisdom and way with words.

I thank my children, Simon and Rachel, and grandson Morgan, for delighting me with their creativity.

I also thank the team at Exisle Publishing for their belief in the book and their guidance.

References

Chapter One

Dalai Lama & Cutler, H. (2000), *The Art of Happiness*, Griffin Press, Adelaide.

Grant, A. & Green, J. (2001), *Coach Yourself: Make real change in your life*, Pearson Education Ltd, London.

Harris, R. (2007), *The Happiness Trap*, Exisle Publishing, Wollombi, NSW.

Sher, Barbara (1996), *Live the Life You Love*, Hodder & Stoughton, Sydney.

Chapter Two

Boldt, Laurence (1999), *Zen and the Art of Making a Living*, Penguin/Arkana, New York.

Cook-Greuter, S.R. & Miller, M. (2000), *Creativity, Spirituality, and Transcendence: Paths to integrity and wisdom in the mature self*, Ablex Publishing Corporation, Connecticut.

Evans, Peter & Deehan, Geoff (1988), *The Keys to Creativity*, Grafton Books, London.

Robinson, Ken (2010), *The Element: How finding your passion changes everything*, Penguin Books, London.

Chapter Four

Charlotte, S. (1993), *Creativity: Conversations with 28 who excel*, Momentum Books Ltd, Michigan.

Evans, Peter & Deehan, Geoff (1988), *The Keys to Creativity*, Grafton Books, London.

Weisburg, Robert (1993), *Creativity: Beyond the myth of genius*, W.H. Freemand and Company, New York.

Chapter Five

Stewart, I. & Joines, V. (1987), *T.A. Today*, Lifespace Publishing, Nottingham.

Chapter Six

Stewart, I. & Joines, V. (1987), *T.A. Today*, Lifespace Publishing, Nottingham.

Chapter Seven

Illsley Clarke, J. (1978), S*elf-Esteem: A family affair*, Harper & Row, San Francisco.

Jeffers, Susan (1987), *Feel the Fear and Do it Anyway*, Century Hutchinson Ltd, London.

Montgomery, B. & Evans, L. (1984), *You and Stress: A guide to successful living*, Nelson Publishers, Melbourne.

Chapter Eight

Grant, A. & Green, J. (2001), *Coach Yourself: Make real change in your life*, Pearson Education Ltd, London.

Chapter Nine

Jones, Tiffany (2003), 'The World Through Water-coloured Glasses — Barry McCann', *Artist's Palette* No. 24

Chapter Eleven

Antony, M. & Swinson, R. (1998), *When Perfect Isn't Good Enough*, New Harbinger Publications, Oakland.

Sallis, Eva, in *Writers on Writing*, Radio National, April 2004.

Chapter Twelve

Csikszentmihalyi, Mihaly (1996), *Creativity: Flow and the psychology of discovery and invention*, Harper Perennial, New York.

Harris, R. (2007), *The Happiness Trap*, Exisle Publishing, Wollombi, NSW.

Kabat-Zinn, Jon (1990), *Full Catastrophe Living*, Piatkus Publishers, London.

Chapter Thirteen

Murray, R. & Zentner, J. (1989), *Nursing Concepts for Health Promotion*, Prentice Hall, London.

Index